Seeking God:
a memoir

Maureen Hallinan
with Ann Primus Berends

ALLIANCE FOR CATHOLIC EDUCATION PRESS
at the University of Notre Dame

Notre Dame, Indiana

Copyright @2015

Alliance for Catholic Education
University of Notre Dame
107 Carole Sandner Hall
Notre Dame, IN 46556
http://ace.nd.edu

Cover design: Mary Jo Adams Kocovski
Interior text layout: Brianna Dombo and
    Mary Jo Adams Kocovski

Library of Congress Cataloging-in-Publication Data

Hallinan, Maureen T.
  Seeking God : a memoir / Maureen Hallinan, with Ann Primus Berends
     pages cm
  ISBN 978-1-935788-11-9
1. Hallinan, Maureen T. 2. Catholics--Biography-- United States. I. Title.
  BX4705.H1375A3 2015
  282.092--dc23
  [B]
                          2014049126

Table of Contents

Introduction

This memoir emerged when Maureen Hallinan was in the final stages of Parkinsonism. Initially, she asked me to write a book with her about two of our spiritual heroes, Thomas Merton and St. John of the Cross. But as weekly sessions turned to daily ones, Maureen's mind turned increasingly to her own spiritual journey. Within a month, we agreed that the book should be in her voice and, through the colorful stories of her life, speak to the Christian's experience—both dark and light—of God. Over the next many weeks, we spent hours together, she talking and I writing, in what became for both of us an invigorating walk on holy ground.

Maureen pursued God tirelessly through life's routines and through life-changing trauma. In her story, this one-time religious sister, brilliant professor, wife, and mother lays bare the mysteries of unabated spiritual hunger, the silence of God, suffering, and death. As a mathematician, she's wired to find the answers. But as she nears the end of her life, still searching for and puzzled by the God she loves, her simple refrain becomes, "I don't know."

Funny, feisty, and uncompromising, she says, "I ask God these questions, and you know what he or she answers? Absolutely nothing." With characteristic dryness, she adds, "Now what kind of friend is that?"

Raised in Queens, New York, the daughter of Irish immigrants is committed to the Church, but continues to struggle with it. She longs to be holy, but never gains the confidence that in Christ she is already holy. She hungers to know deeply the generous love of Jesus as Merton and John of the Cross describe it. But she never quite grasps it.

Her contemplative life is marked more by a sense of darkness than of light. Her prayer life is marked more by a sense of divine silence than divine presence. Her earthly life is marked more by a sense of professional success than of the gentle goodness she desires.

Still, she remains faithful, because God is faithful.

This is the story of Maureen Hallinan, a devout Catholic skeptic who navigated women's rights and family life with equal resolve; fought her way through personal torture and domestic tragedy with relentless courage; and wrestled with God with indefatigable fury, as if to say, like Jacob, "I will not let go until you bless me."

She writes, "I seem like such an odd duck to myself. I don't think I'm like normal people." But struggling believers who read her story will see otherwise. She speaks for all of us.

APB, August 2013

If you are seeking God, you can be sure of this:
God is seeking you much more.
(St. John of the Cross, Living Flame of Love*)*

I
Beginning Again, April 2013

It's hard to believe that I am living in the Helen Schubert Assisted Living facility of Holy Cross Village, Notre Dame. I had no expectation of developing a serious neurological illness at an early age. And I did not expect to terminate my academic career at what feels like a premature age. And yet, with strong encouragement from my family and friends, this is where I find myself.

Am I happy here? It is too soon to know. I have now been here for a month, most of which has been spent settling in, learning the names of people with whom I share no history, plans, or goals. This is not what I anticipated.

To understand my emotional reaction to this unexpected situation, one would need to know how I expected the last part of my life to play out.

I intended to be a nun again.

It used to be highly respected among Irish families to have at least one child pursue the religious life. Irish mothers took this very seriously and promoted the value of the calling. Mine was no different. So from a very early age I thought about becoming a nun. It had such meaning attached to it. It meant that I was from a good Catholic family that practiced Catholicism seriously. It also meant that God loved me, that I was a special person in the Army of Christ. (We are called the Fighting Irish for a reason.) I can remember that I very much wanted to love God and this was the way the Church and my family were telling me to do that.

In my family there were a lot of expectations about how one lived and behaved, and what one thought about. We didn't talk about it; I just absorbed these expectations by osmosis. I didn't need anyone to put God or questions of God in my head. It was in the air we breathed at home and in the Catholic religion we were taught in school.

So when I turned fifteen, I sought my parents' permission to become a nun when I graduated from high school. They gladly gave it. I did not initially mention to them that I wanted to become a Carmelite nun, living in a cloistered community dedicated to prayer. I was contemplatively oriented, though I did not know enough to call it that at the time. I thought everybody was fascinated by questions about God.

When I finally did reveal my desire to become a Carmelite, my dad objected, arguing that it was too strenuous a life for me and would damage my health.

Convinced he would not relent, I decided to enter the Religious of the Sacred Heart of Mary, an order whose mission is education.

I spent my first year after high school as a postulant, learning how to live a religious life. I then entered the novitiate to continue my religious and academic training. Over three years, I adopted the lifestyle of a nun and completed a college degree.

After seventeen years, I left my religious community. By then I had earned my Ph.D. and secured my first university job. Soon thereafter, I got married and had two children. But sometime along the way—I'm not sure when—I thought of becoming a nun again. It was just there in the back of my mind. I thought I would know when it was time to go back to religious life. I would complete my avocations toward the people I love, finish my responsibilities toward my family and my students, and become a nun again.

Initially, my motivation was that I wanted to be like the person I was when I first entered religious life, inspired by obedience to my parents and the Church. That's no longer true. Now, I simply want to be someone who loves God passionately, and the religious framework can help me release this longing, this desire to be with God, and help me connect with him or her in a new way.

This plan, if you can call it that, has not always been in my mind consciously, particularly during the liveliest part of my life, when my husband and I were full of energy and strength and the excitement of participating in family and professional life. But God has always been a major presence to me. My consciousness of him or her has not been built on theology or practice, but even in my darkest days—which have been numerous—there has been a dull awareness of God, of ritual, sacrament, and the sorts of things that God cares about.

Obviously, I will not be a nun again. So I have decided to make Holy Cross Village my setting for finding God and for prayer.

I always have been attracted to prayer, yet I may be one of the world's least competent pray-ers. I say that because the way other people pray really doesn't appeal to me. I don't engage in long, cerebral prayers; they sound like literary analysis to me. I'm thirsty to pray, but I do not feel that I know how to do it. Or I don't do it well. Now I'm at Holy Cross Village and I think, Here I am again, trying to learn how to pray. I might flunk out.

But I keep at it. Every day I walk the halls and I pray. Every single time I go down the corridor, I am thinking about God. I say to him or her, "I will talk to you every day." You know what he or she answers? Absolutely nothing. What am I supposed to do with a friend like that? Maybe I have the wrong image of God.

I keep at it. When I get up, I get dressed; I cannot think when I'm getting dressed because that takes too much concentration. I get through it slowly. My mind starts waking up when I walk down to the dining room, and then I think about God. I think about how wonderful it is, these stories we have been told and how wonderful it would be if they were true. And then I remind myself: they *are* true. I believe these stories, and I am going to live as if I do. This process of awakening begins every single day.

What I'm learning is that the life of pursuing God, of prioritizing God, is more than we imagine it to be. It is everything. It is all we can do.

You do not need to know precisely what is happening, or exactly where it is all going. What you need is to recognize the possibilities and challenges offered by the present moment, and to embrace them with courage, faith, and hope. (*Thomas Merton,* Conjectures of a Guilty Bystander)

II

(Not Your Average)
Irish Catholic Girl

My parents came from Ireland as teenagers, not so much because they were poor but because America was the "land of opportunity." At the time, I think that there was no such thing as being poor in Ireland. From my perspective, yes, they were poor. But from theirs, they were just like everyone else. What mattered to Irish parents was that they get their children to America so they could secure a successful future.

My mother had relatives of some means in the U.S. They invited her and her sister to live with them so my mother and her sister could expand their experience of life and learn the things they would need to know to become employed as maids or babysitters. My mother had great skills as a maid. She knew all the etiquette and passed that on to us: how to set a perfect table, starch and iron a shirt, polish silver. Nothing I ever used.

My father came to the States as a teen. He had no relatives here except a distant uncle, which is significant only in that the uncle was a bartender during the days of

Prohibition and had a reputation that went beyond even that. My dad was a holy man, a good man, so he avoided this uncle. He took a job as a milk carrier and did other small jobs; he took anything he could get.

I grew up during WWII; society was changing because of the war, and the turnover of jobs was enormous. By the time he had a family, my father had gone through a number of jobs that lasted only as long as the employers could employ him. Finally he found a job working as a motorman in the New York City subway system. It was a good job because it gave him exemption from the war until the very end of the war, when he was too old to fight. The job paid well. And it had status because it was viewed by the government as so necessary to the well-being of the country that you didn't have to go to war. He earned a good salary, and motorman became his life-long profession.

I used to worry that my dad would lose his health living underground all the time, but he didn't. It wasn't an easy job. In fact, I think it was a lot harder than he let us know because he wanted to protect his family in this foreign country. The trains weren't as good then as now, so often there were accidents or suicides. If people fell or threw themselves on the tracks, the motorman could not stop the train. He was simply given a day or two off to recover from the ordeal. I didn't learn about that until he told me much later.

Earlier on he told us a wonderful story that I hold close to my heart. One day my father had to stop the train between two stations because something was on the track up ahead. He had to wait for the signal to start again. It didn't come for the longest time. Finally he got out of the train and went down on the tracks to see what was happening. However, he couldn't see because he was too far from whatever was blocking the path.

As my father waited, he was thinking of his family, and he drew a heart on the subway wall in the dust with the names of his children inside. Many years later he told me, "Did you know your names are written on the subway wall?" He told me the story with such pride and such pleasure. I interpreted it as saying, "I love you so much, my family, that I can't stop thinking of you." His simple inscription was so beautiful and demonstrated his goodness. He was a major figure in my life. I adored my father, and we were very close. He was exceptional.

My mother stayed home with us full time. She had a heavy touch. What she wanted most for each of her children was that we go to heaven and that we be highly educated along the way. Do I remember hearing those words from her? No, not per se. But I just knew it. My mother was such a powerful personality that you knew what her values were without having to be told. And you knew that if you violated her values, you would experience her wrath.

My siblings will tell you that I am much like her, but I don't believe it.

My mother was very strict; she was difficult and demanding and critical of everybody. You weren't around her without being criticized, either to your face or to others. She wasn't a bad woman. She tried hard to be good, but she didn't have the apparatus to win social points. Her goal was to raise good children whose lives were consistent with what we were taught in church by the priests and in school by the nuns. And she got her wish; we all turned out to be good students, good people.

My mother was a proud woman who put a lot of emphasis on academics. She tried to help us with our homework when we were very young, but because she had little education herself, she didn't know how. She must have felt like a failure in that regard, though of course she never communicated anything of the sort. That would have been putting herself down, and she would find that intolerable.

Fortunately, we were all pretty smart, and in my case I didn't need to be told to study. I loved to study. Still, it was hard to meet her expectations, even when I wanted what she wanted of me. I wasn't the shining star she wanted me to be. I wanted to be close to her, but I wasn't. You'd have to give up much of yourself to please her, and I was too independent to do that.

My image of God developed more from my mother than from my father, I suppose because she was home with us, and in those days raising children and imposing values on them was the mother's job. She had full access to us, and she exercised it.

That said, my father was the primary influence on my spiritual formation. He was gentle, kind, loving, playful. He had a certitude about faith that people long for. I have so many memories of watching my dad sitting in a living room chair reading books by Thomas Merton. My father revered Thomas Merton. He once met him; it may have been the high point of his life.

More than once I squirreled away two or three of those books by Merton to my bedroom. I was enthralled by his words. I knew I wasn't fully grasping my father's understanding of God or his attraction to the goodness of God as Thomas Merton captured it in his books. But I so wanted to have that goodness. Of course, I was eventually caught with those stolen treasures. My father asked me why I was so attracted to the writings of Thomas Merton. This was thrilling for me, that my father was interested in my interest in the person who fascinated him.

Both of my parents died years ago, but they still live in my mind every single day.

I was the second child in our family of four children—
John, me, Tom, and Rita. Until I was six years old, we
lived in an apartment in Woodside, New York, which is
famous for nothing except it housed the Bulova Watch
Factory. That fascinated all of us; we didn't know what
happened in factories.

We rented our apartment from a Russian couple who
had two boys. The couple spoke English and Russian
and they were generous and kind and very good to my
poor immigrant parents, who as Irish people didn't even
consider trying to integrate themselves into American
society. All they cared about was that their children
would become good American citizens, and that they
were good Catholics.

When I was in first grade, we left the apartment in
Woodside and settled in a house in Flushing—another
Queens neighborhood. We were not proud of coming
from Flushing; it was the basis of something else that,
like our parents' Irish brogues, the American kids
could tease us about. What do you do in Flushing? We
flush. We thought it was highly offensive to come from
Flushing.

Our house was originally a two-family, one apartment
up and one down, that we converted into a three-family,
with two apartments upstairs. We lived on the main

floor and in the basement. Aunt Katherine and Uncle Johnny lived next door to us. Their house was a two-family. Uncle Johnny was a plumber, and he taught my dad all the plumbing that he knew, which was a big help.

Uncle Johnny was also something of a drinker. (Weren't we all?) Aunt Katherine and Uncle Johnny lived a pretty peaceful life until Friday evenings. He never came home on time on a Friday. Never. Aunt Katherine would get very upset about this. Living next door to them you could look out the window into their kitchen and see pots and pans being thrown around and hear the yelling. My brother John and I got a kick out of it. Every single Friday, we would stand at the window and watch those fireworks.

On the other side of our house was an Italian family that we didn't talk to, because in those days the Irish and the Italians did not mix. We didn't even look at each other much. In that house lived the grandparents, one or two sets of parents, and one little boy, Johnny. He was the youngest of the children on the block. He was constantly trying to horn in on our gang, but we didn't let him. Still he kept coming around.

Down the block lived a family of little people—one woman and three men. They worked in the circus; I thought that was fascinating. They practiced walking the tightrope in the vacant lot next to their house. One day after school, when I knew they weren't at home, I took myself down to the lot and started walking on the tightrope. My mother saw me and shouted, "Oh my god, that's Maureen!" But before she could get to me, I scrambled down and disappeared out of sight. I knew how to escape trouble.

My brother John was the kingpin of neighborhood shenanigans. He was a rascal, and inventive, and he could get us behind an idea in no time. One afternoon we saw the movie Joan of Arc. A day or two later, we were playing in the lot down the block, which was filled with trees and poison ivy and who knows what else. After a short while, little Johnny came to play with us.

My brother said, "Hey, come to the back of the lot, Johnny. We're gonna teach you a new game." Then we tied him to a tree and said, "Did you see the movie about the life of Joan of Arc? She was very brave, so brave that she was arrested by the bad guys, who tied her to a tree and burned her. That's what we're going to do to you, Johnny."

Little Johnny started bawling. It was terrible, just terrible. Somebody started screaming when they had the match lit and ready to burn the trees. One of the neighbors came running and whisked Johnny away. He wasn't hurt, but he was terrified, of course, because of how mean these kids were, including myself.

✝ ✝ ✝

Sometimes my parents fought. Not all the time, but enough to give me heartburn. My stomach would clench when my mother got started.

Her behavior created tension between us siblings, though that tension was a topic she studiously avoided discussing with us. She was so hard on us that I felt I needed an ally. I couldn't ask John. He was an adversarial person, and if I said, "John, help me deal with Mom on this issue," he would say no simply because I asked him.

My younger brother, on the other hand, was a sweetheart, and he became my ally. This was unfair in a way because I was asking him to help me with issues that I was probably better equipped to handle; I was four-and-a-half years older, after all. But my mother drove me to do that. I needed an ally.

One of the terrible memories I have is when John did something to upset my parents. He was in eighth grade, a cute little redhead, and mischievous. At my mother's strong insistence, my father took the belt to him. It bothered Tom and me immensely that John should be dealt such a humiliation.

This may have been the first time that I thought perhaps I hated my mother. We children were so profoundly offended that the memory has stayed with each of us over the years. I think that says good things about my parents, but also bad things. They could have gotten us together and said, "Let's talk about this." It was a serious event that affected the whole family. But they didn't. It wasn't our way to talk things through. It still isn't my way.

A beating like that never happened again. I think my brothers steered clear of my father from that point on, which is why they were never as close to him as I was. It also played into our relationship with each other. How, I don't know. But I can't help believing it did.

Overall, I think our family was not healthy psychologically. All those unarticulated feelings needed to be explored, especially by young children who didn't have the sophistication and explication to do it themselves. We could have learned so much about ourselves and each other by talking about it with an adult who understood, but we never did. We were very private. We didn't talk about our feelings.

We did, however, laugh a lot. Laughter was a big part of our household, and it has always been important to me. Most visits from relatives ended with a meal and then gathering to tell stories for the rest of the evening. "Let's move into the living room," someone would say. One or the other of us would start. There would be libations throughout, so it got louder and funnier (we thought).

We covered a lot of territory, the whole family, adults, grandparents, babies, telling and listening to stories. The funniest were always from my father and my cousin Mary Jo's father, Uncle Tom.

I wonder why we don't think of God laughing. Why doesn't our religion emphasize that? I cannot picture God the Father laughing. Jesus, I can see laughing sometimes. As for the Holy Spirit, it's hard to think of him as laughing, because doves don't laugh.

When my mother was pregnant with my younger brother, she did not share the news with my older brother or me. But we noticed. I went out and made an announcement to all the neighbors. My Irish mother, who didn't ever talk about sex, not with her kids, not with anyone, was most unhappy about this publicity. So she lied about it. "I am not pregnant," she said.

Now I was smart enough to know that lying about the pregnancy would become a problem, and this worried me. When my mother had the baby, we would have to hide it. I was relieved when she finally admitted the truth. John and I were given strict orders not to talk about it. I can't imagine what she thought we were going to say. At any rate, John and I decided we would not talk to *her* about it. We never mentioned it in front of her again, though we took every opportunity to talk about it at school and other places.

When I was in elementary school, I remember being astonished that some people in the world did not believe in God. How could they be so dumb? But this worried me, too. Then I had what can only be described as an epiphany. My Aunt Delia—who was actually my mother's first cousin—never married. She was my mother's age, a very quiet, nice lady. I realized that, if God were God, he or she would give Aunt Delia a baby. And if God gave her a baby, it would prove to the world that God exists, because Aunt Delia would have a baby without having a husband. I didn't tell Aunt Delia that I understood this of course, but I told the nun in school. I said that my aunt was going to have a baby and that she should tell the other children because then they'll know there is a God.

Growing up, I was especially close to my cousin Mary Jo. We were born three days apart, she the older and I the younger. That stigma of being "the youngest" has lived on. For seventy-three years, Mary Jo has emphasized that I am the less experienced, the less knowledgeable, the less everything she can think of.

The day she was born, Uncle Tom sent a short telegram to my father, paying a penny per word: "Baby girl mother and baby doing fine." Three days later I was born and my dad one-upped him with a shorter telegram that said, "Ditto." Uncle Tom saved that telegram.

Mary Jo lived in New Jersey, but we visited each other every Thanksgiving and certain other occasions during the year. I loved her. I thought she was perfect and beautiful and smart. I feel very lucky to have gotten her as a cousin. We're in touch to this day. I got three notes from her this past week.

My mother's mother often came from Ireland to visit. I liked my Grams, as we called her, though most of the family did not. She had this tendency to come to the States a little too often, which was expensive for the family, and she caused trouble between husbands and wives. We were the last ones to get her after the others couldn't handle her any longer. But I liked her. I thought she was very nice.

She stayed in my room during her visits. Every afternoon at 4:00 pm, she'd tap on something and when my mother appeared, she would say, "I'm thirsty." My mother knew what that meant. So she would fetch her a shot glass full of whiskey. Grams would always say, "Oh, that's too much." But after a pause, she would add, "Well, nobody wants to drink this after I've touched it, so you may as well leave it." Every day this was the routine. My mother would put a little doily under the shot glass because that made it more festive. Then my mother would go in with her tea and they would drink together. At some point my mother thought there must be something to this whiskey, so she'd have a shot, too.

Grams would go back to Ireland and stay until she couldn't stand the loneliness anymore. She ended up dying in the States, though she wanted to be buried in Ireland next to her husband. So many people say they want to be buried next to their spouses. Isn't that strange? Who cares? Certainly not your spouse!

I found elementary and middle school so easy that I didn't have to spend much time on my studies. But by the time I got to high school, I found learning so interesting that I studied much of the time. I would never trade my schoolwork for play because I loved it so much.

At the end of middle school, I skipped half a grade, ending in January instead of in the spring, and started my freshman year of high school that same month. My mother enrolled me in a school that her aunt, a nun, was affiliated with. It was a point of pride for my mother to put her allegedly genius daughter into her aunt's school.

We didn't have enough money to send the four of us to a Catholic high school, but my parents would not think of sending us to public school, so my dad took on extra jobs. He continued to work in the subway and he also worked as a guard at the factory. He picked up janitorial work when I was in high school; for that job, my dad wore a uniform that he hated. He called it his "monkey suit." I worried about how much he was working. So I used to go with him and help him empty trash and do other things so that he could go home and get some sleep. We became even closer during this time because we chatted about different things in our commute from home to factory.

In those days, the diocese offered scholarships to the all-girls and all-boys high schools in New York. I applied for a few. The first one I did not get because I didn't show all of my work on the math problems. I got the answers right, but I didn't show my work. If there was anything I knew, it was math, so it was astonishing that I did not get that scholarship. I was crushed.

I took a test for another full scholarship from the Transport Workers Union, which my dad belonged to. Some little kid who was brighter than me got the full scholarship. I won a half scholarship, but I felt miserable because they presented the scholarships in front of these motormen, and I didn't get the full. This was my father's union and I wanted to make him proud. In the end, I did get scholarships in my sophomore, junior, and senior years.

My high school was called the Academy of the Sacred Heart of Mary. It was in the Bronx, an hour's journey from my house in Flushing. I had to take two buses to get there, but that didn't bother me. It was a very pleasant trip. Before boarding the bus for school, I would go to daily mass. My parents went to mass every morning and I decided high school was a good time for me to take on this holy practice, too. This meant I could eat no breakfast at home—it's important to observe a "fast" as a way of preparing for the Holy Eucharist—so I boiled myself an egg to eat on the bus. Caesar and Cicero are hard to do on an empty stomach. But you can only eat so many boiled eggs; to this day, I hate boiled eggs.

Studying and learning were fascinating to me, and I loved the independence of the process. I could turn on the information well to any channel I chose and weave it together the way I chose. I found learning anything fascinating, even as a young girl. I loved to read, I loved to study; I'd pick up anything and read it, and then link it to other things. Even on Saturdays, I would ride the two buses to my high school so that I could take extra classes. Did my parents think this was unusual behavior for a young girl? I don't know, but they did think of me as smart, and this pleased me.

My friends were not the most popular kids in the class, but we were all well liked. The most popular kids came from the Bronx because that was where the school was. They could stay after school for clubs and athletics. I did become editor of the school paper and the yearbook. I never felt ostracized; I wasn't thought of as a showoff.

Most of us liked the school, each other, and the teachers. It was a pretty happy place.

When I started at the Academy, my mother told the principal that I would one day be the valedictorian. The principal told her he did not believe so; there were many smart girls in the school, he said, and two of the smartest girls who had ever enrolled in the school were in my class. But in my senior year, along with the general excellence medal and the mathematics medal, I became valedictorian. "Mother knows best," as they say.

In September of 1957—I was seventeen—I entered religious life, spending the first half year as a postulant and then one year as a novice. I studied at Marymount College Tarrytown, an all-girls, pre-K through college campus on the Hudson River, about an hour's drive from downtown Manhattan. Marymount was founded by the religious order I belonged to, Religious of the Sacred Heart of Mary; not long ago it became a part of Fordham University.

For the first eighteen months we lived in community but were separated from the professed nuns. (We might contaminate them.) For the first six months we were also separated from the other students. (They might contaminate us.) Then we attended classes with them, but we weren't allowed to speak to them. Still, I liked that period of time.

This was a French community and when you first entered, you were called Mademoiselle and then Madame. I wanted to take the name Therese, after St. Therese, the Little Flower. St. Therese was a Carmelite nun who "scattered flowers," as she called it, through small deeds of kindness. She chose that kind of ministry because she was so bad at it. She was proud and liked the accolades that came from doing the big good deeds. I can relate to that. But another nun already had the name Therese. Then I wanted to be Madame Lefleuwrdejesu (Little Flower of Jesus), but someone else had taken that name, if you can believe it. So I became Marie Teresita.

After I entered the community, I realized all nuns were not equally serious about religious life. You might think, "How can you not take it seriously? It's such a dramatic life choice." But for some, morning prayers walking the grounds may have been nothing more than an opportunity to watch the squirrels. I know because I took that opportunity. I found that a wonderful thing to do, though I felt guilty about it. I learned a lot about squirrels because, as I said, I have never been much good at prayer.

During our study of spirituality I became enamored of John of the Cross. He seemed the ultimate to me, because he was a contemplative. He was *the* contemplative. I never saw him as a stern or rigid person, the way many people characterize him. He had a profound influence on Thomas Merton, so my father loved him, and that was enough for me. I started reading him with more seriousness of purpose when I became a nun.

I remember trying to understand the Divine Office, the set of prayers that the Church wants us to recite throughout the day. It became difficult for me to understand why religious attached so much importance to it. Because I found God fascinating, I expected to find the Office fascinating, but I didn't. I found it distasteful. It quotes the Old Testament frequently, and the Old Testament has always been difficult for me to understand. It doesn't present God the way John of the Cross does—as an insanely loving being. To be faced with this document that has so many pieces that do not depict God as particularly loving baffled me. I never overcame that lack of understanding.

Discipline was harsh in the convent. Because we lived under the rule of silence, we were not supposed to talk to each other except during recreation period, which was a half hour once a day after dinner. If we broke the rule, we might be told, "Madame, kiss the floor fifty times." We didn't always think of it as punishment, though, because it gave us something to laugh about. I remember once when my friend and I were both told to kiss the floor; at one point I looked over at her, and we burst into laughter. We were just young kids, really, and we did things that young people do—laugh and tease each other and the like. So we took quite lightly some of the rules and structure under which we lived.

Sometimes you were given a penance. We learned many prayers in Latin and some in French. If I whispered something to my buddy before the allowed time (I got caught, always), the Mistress of Novices would give me a penalty. She was the one in charge of making us holy, which meant suffering, and she would say, "Your penalty is to say the Miserere on the floor with your arms outstretched before you may go to dinner." That gets hard after a while, especially if you can't remember the Miserere, which is all of Psalm 51. You had to do this in front of everyone; that deepened the humiliation, you see. And then worse, when you couldn't remember it, you became known as the novice who couldn't remember the Miserere. All your friends had to wait to eat dinner until your penance was over. I think I got it after the fourth or fifth time.

After eighteen months, I became a novice; this is when I got my habit and made my first vows. That was a big day for someone in the religious life. My parents attended. Just before the service, my mother said "You know you don't have to enter the convent." I was furious because part of me didn't really want to enter the convent. I thought, Lady, why didn't you say that to me a year ago?

(Not Your Average) Irish Catholic Girl   33

I wouldn't have done it. Still, I took my vows that day because I was certain God wanted me to. But I was very angry with my mother for a long time.

I graduated college in 1961.

*In order to understand God, we cannot
leap to our own understanding,
but must seek God and wait . . .
For the Spirit is living and full of meaning,
far more than literal words themselves,
and it has the miraculous ability to affect lives
far beyond all we can imagine or expect.
(St. John of the Cross,* Ascent of Mount
Carmel*)*

III
Habit Life

After college I was sent to teach in an all-girls Catholic boarding school in Sag Harbor, on the eastern tip of Long Island. The school included pre-K through senior high; girls of all ages boarded. Some local students who were not boarders also attended the school. There were just over 300 students in all. I was assigned to teach math in the high school, though occasionally it was necessary to fill in at a lower level.

I loved teaching from the start. Probably before I was born I had a ruler in my hand—not to beat kids with, but as a tool to teach them math. In looking back at that time, it is interesting to me now that I did not know I loved teaching before being assigned to the school. But day by day it grew on me, understanding the potential of the impact I could have on students' lives by the gift that I'd been given. It thrilled me to see the goodness of the fit of teaching with sharing my insights about God with students. That conviction came to me as a great privilege and a huge responsibility, but one that I gladly embraced.

Having a younger sister the age of my students kept me grounded in the realities of their lives. Whether the students paid much attention to my reality, I don't know. I do know it was important to me that they come to a deeper understanding of God. It pleased me immensely that I was part of that process.

These were students who were in high school during the tumultuous social period that preceded the Civil Rights movement. It wasn't quite so peaceful as many people picture it today. I had already seen change brewing when I was a senior in high school. There was one black girl, Dorabelle, in my class of about sixty students. For a senior year trip we went to Washington D.C. On the way down we stopped at a popular chain restaurant for lunch. The two nuns in charge of the trip went into the restaurant first and talked to the manager about letting Dorabelle into the restaurant. He said no. So the nuns said, "If she doesn't come in, the bus load doesn't come in." Dorabelle was a beloved student, and my fellow students and I didn't agree with the restaurant. This is where some of the rebellion was beginning.

The girls in Sag Harbor seemed so uninterested in the things that captured my imagination and heart. Yet I didn't blame them for that. I attributed it to their age and inexperience. I kept in mind that the students were young and were growing up in a different culture with different values from mine. They were from different socioeconomic backgrounds, many from well-to-do families, most of whom were involved in acting. Some were at the other end of the distribution—local girls who didn't board and paid their tuition in potatoes or ducks or liquor. They were like all kids: they didn't think about God. Or, I didn't think they thought about God. They were interested in boys and dress, and I was never interested in that. That kind of stuff seemed dumb to me.

I loved celebrating May Day. We'd dress up in long dresses and dance across the lawn and sing hymns to Our Lady and throw flowers and run around the Maypole with ribbons. I like Mary. Always have. She's humble, and people who aren't humble drive me nuts because they think they've given themselves their gifts, rather than receiving them from God. What kind of nonsense is that? But Mary, she was just a simple, humble woman who was gifted in special ways and believed these spirits that she spoke to.

I began every class I taught with a short prayer to the Holy Spirit because I wanted my students to come to see him as a spirit of love and wisdom: "Come Holy Spirit, fill the hearts of your faithful and kindle in them the fire of your love. Send forth your Spirit and they shall be created. And you shall renew the face of the earth. O God, who by the light of the Holy Spirit did instruct the hearts of the faithful, grant that by the same Holy Spirit we may be truly wise and ever enjoy his consolations. Through Christ Our Lord, Amen."

That's very powerful. I said it every day for years. The kids had to say it with me. My hope was that it would bring to their attention a loving image of God. Every year a small portion of them would enter religious life. That pleased me.

I would become impatient when students didn't want to learn or did not work hard. That infuriated me. I've been teased over the years for being tough on people; using "the stare" I learned from the nuns in my elementary school. I don't deny that. I am not tender, and I have brought graduate students to tears. But that wouldn't be the first thing I would talk about if I were talking about myself as a teacher. I would talk about how, as a student myself, I loved learning math and I wanted to learn all the math I could possibly learn. I was very ambitious. I could not understand kids that didn't want to learn. And I would talk about how, when I was in Sag Harbor, I taught geometry to the slowest students and almost all of them passed. That was unheard of in those days. I truly did love teaching, and I loved teaching math.

I was a good teacher—with two exceptions: a senior physics class and a junior prep class for the SAT. I taught physics the first year I taught, the first day I taught. I had never had physics, ever; never took it, did anything with it, wouldn't have cared less if I had never heard about physics, and here I was teaching it my very first day. Oh dear God! I taught myself what I could by studying the New York State Regents' exam answer book. Everyone had to take that exam to get to the next class, so I hoped it would help me stay one step ahead of the students.

One student asked, "My father wants to know how you conclude that the birds on electric wires don't get electrocuted." Good question. It didn't make any sense to me how that's possible. I made up something outlandish, but I knew I was overstepping my bounds. She brought the message home to her father, and the next day I had a phone call asking me to explain what I had taught his daughter about the birds. I mumbled something, thinking, God has punished me. That father gave up on me.

I gave up on the class, too. One day while I was writing on the board, the students slowly moved their desks up toward me until I was literally pinned against the wall. The bell rang, and I couldn't leave. It was really scary. Finally out of pity they let me out. I walked out of the classroom, down the hall, and out of the building. My principal came after me and eventually persuaded me to stay. I turned around, went back to class, got my New York Regents book, and started studying again. I still don't understand how it is those birds don't get electrocuted.

When Ethel and Julius Rosenberg were convicted in 1951 for selling secrets about the atomic bomb to the Russians, they were sentenced to death—by electrocution wouldn't you know. Julius got electrocuted first, then Ethel. I told my physics class that it took 100 volts of electricity to electrocute him and 300 to electrocute her. They asked why it took so much more to electrocute her than him. It made no sense to me, but I couldn't say that to them. So I said, "Well, you know they didn't talk much about it," and rushed on to something else.

Later that day, another interested father called and asked if I could please explain the electrocution of Ethel and Julius Rosenberg to him. And I said, "You know, they didn't give out a lot of information about that execution because of the controversy and I don't know any more about it than that." The father accepted that, but the girls were smart enough to know better.

I was never asked to teach physics again, thank God.

But then they asked me to teach preparation for the SAT. I thought, easy, the SAT is common sense. Ha. I went to the first class and, hells bells, I didn't know anything. I didn't know any of the answers. I just couldn't relate to it. Not too many of my students passed at an acceptable level. I resolved to do better. The next semester I taught the same course to different students but with the same results. So they dropped the course.

My third year of teaching at Sag Harbor, I started going to summer school at Adelphi, a fairly big university on

Long Island. I took courses there over two summers. I loved the classes but hated the experience. Nobody would talk to me, probably because I wore a habit. So I would slip into class at the last minute as a way of avoiding having to be ignored. And after class I would disappear.

When I won a fellowship for teachers of high school math from the National Science Foundation, my community slated me to be a scholar. After six years in Sag Harbor, they sent me to the University of Notre Dame.

✝ ✝ ✝

I started a master's program in math at Notre Dame, assuming that when I completed it I'd go back and teach high school math again. But then my community insisted I go on for a Ph.D. So I got a fellowship and met with the chair of Notre Dame's math department to discuss the program. Turns out he had no interest in welcoming a woman into the ranks. He urged me not to take the fellowship and said, "You won't like it here. There's not much talking in math, you know." As if women have to talk all the time. Sexist. But when the chair of the department you want to enter suggests that you not enter, you no longer want to enter. So I left math.

The University of Chicago had also offered me a fellow-ship for a three-year Ph.D. program in education. I took it, thinking, Great, I'll get my degree and then I'll go back to teaching high school.

I studied for a year and a half, took the preliminary exams, and did very well. The chair of the education department suggested I take other courses in the social sciences. At that point I didn't even know what those courses would be, so when he asked me about it, I said rather lamely, "I do like people." He suggested I take psychology courses, so I took those cross-listed with sociology, not really understanding what I was doing. I did well in the exams in those areas. I didn't like psychology as well as sociology because it was too experimental. So I finally pursued a joint Ph.D. in sociology and education.

The University of Chicago was a lively, challenging, amazing place to be. And to be one of the few women there helped change my image of myself. I learned how to be a woman in a man's world, and how to take advantage of it. A reasonable woman who did not say stupid things was treated nicely, if not equally. She was appointed to committees and included on boards. She was given something of a voice.

This was the beginning of the women's movement, when a large number of people at the university formed the Chicago Women's Liberation Union (CWLU). You would assume that I was part of that union, and some of my best friends in the discipline were active in it—like Terry Sullivan, who is now president of the University of Virginia. But I did not consider myself part of it. I was sympathetic to it, but I was apolitical. I didn't want to gain the reputation of someone who was radical. It wasn't to my advantage.

Even so, the CWLU influenced my career. Many years later I was nominated to be president of the American Sociological Association. This was a big deal. Only five women had served as ASA president since the organization's beginning in 1904. The CWLU formed a questionnaire that they would give to each candidate, and if you gave the wrong answers to questions about women's roles on campus or in a particular discipline, they would not support you. Fortunately, I gave the right answers and I became president.

We had an unprecedented sweep of women officers that year. Felice Levine was already executive director, Myra Marx Ferree was elected vice president, and Terry Sullivan was elected secretary. This irritated many of the older male sociologists. The usual issues of affirmative action were raised, including the suspicion that we were unqualified. One eminent sociologist was overheard saying, "Who are these feminist nobodies?" In response, we had four big "Feminist Nobody" buttons made, which we wore at the annual ASA conference. I think Terry still has hers.

This confidence as a woman and intellectual began building when I was a student at Chicago. Along the way, I lost patience with the Church for its rigidity in so many areas. It had become so conservative. I loved the Church, but I really disliked its backwardness and its impatience with women. Many things had built up and made the Church an anachronism to a lot of young people.

I began to think that I couldn't stay in community anymore. I wanted to serve the Church outside of community. I didn't think I could live as a religious in a habit, a person set apart from the public, in clothes that made it clear that I was a person dedicated to God in some removed way. It took time for me to make the final decision to leave, but that was my frame of mind through the rest of graduate school.

My brother Tom and I became close while I was in graduate school. He was drafted into the military during the Vietnam War, which took a toll on the whole family. While he was in Vietnam, he lost four soldiers in his unit in one day, including his dearest friend, Steve.

When they were recalled, my brother went to Washington where Steve had lived to thank his family for giving Steve to this country. He is still in touch with them. Tom is almost seventy. That's a lot of years to stay in touch with the family of your deceased friend.

Tom came home from Vietnam through Chicago to see me. The first night he was home, I borrowed a house from a faculty member so Tom would have a place that was quiet so that he could rest. I got up the next morning and headed out to pick up bacon and eggs. I didn't see Tom, but I went out anyway, thinking he would appear when I got back.

He did not appear. I became concerned, thinking suicide, and searched every room in the house. I found him under the couch in the living room, where he felt safe from being bombed. You'd have to know Tom. He is a gentle, kind, generous person, and the violence of the war almost killed him. To this day, I ask God, "Why did you do that? Why did you allow that to happen to Tom?"

During my third year at the University of Chicago, I took a course with Marlene Dixon in symbolic interactionism (which studies the words, gestures, and other symbols people rely on when they communicate). Marlene Dixon was one of the firebrands of the uprisings in the '60s, the founder of the Chicago Women's Liberation Union, and a vociferous instigator of rebellion against the administration for its lack of greater involvement in civil rights issues. The university did not want to be perceived as radical; at this time, a number of prestigious universities had spawned strong, rebellious civil rights groups, and Chicago didn't want to become one of them.

I knew very little about Marlene Dixon or her role in the uprisings, but I took the course with her. She was a good teacher, and I found the subject fascinating, especially as it pertained to conversation between people of different races. When she assigned a term paper, I chose the book *Black Like Me* as my subject. Race and justice and equity—these areas were becoming of increasing interest to me.

At this time, I lived with two other women on the first floor of a multi-roomed apartment. One afternoon, I was outside the apartment working on my paper. Two boys walked by—a black boy and a white boy, arms around each other's shoulder. I was enchanted by this; it reminded me of *Black Like Me*.

"What are you doin'?" they asked me. "I'm studying," I said. "Where do you live?" they asked. I pointed to our apartment. They said, "Do you have cookies in there?" So I invited them in to make some with me. You think it would have dawned on me that I was being manipulated.

We made a big batch of chocolate chip cookies and they gobbled them down. A week or so later, their older brothers happened to come along and broke into our apartment. People upstairs saw them. They robbed us, raped us, and tortured us. One of them used a gun to bang me on the head, which bled and did not stop. This made them panic and they left.

The first night after the robbery, the superior of the Jesuit House, where my friend John Rohr lived with about twenty other priests, invited us to stay with them. The next morning when I woke up, my roommate, Sharon, was setting her hair. That struck me as strange. She was very bright, very alive, a fascinating person. I liked her a lot. But we certainly reacted differently to the event. She was worried about her hair, while the most important part of the event to me was, How are we going to handle this? Can we do anything about these men who tortured us, these miserable specimens of humanity who did to us what they did?

God's role in this was not a preoccupation, nor was my sense of personal suffering. I just wanted to get through the experience. I never heard Sharon mention God in connection with it, either. These were intense times, but I kept them separate from my thinking about God because I couldn't imagine the two being linked together.

The news spread like wildfire. I couldn't not think about it even if I wanted to. We went to the police station several times to identify the men in lineups. Sharon had a terrible time with that. There were four bad guys, and she couldn't decide which ones they were. It took a long time.

People were very gentle; they didn't want to disrupt things. A convent of nuns from my community ran a school close to the University of Chicago. After the robbery, they invited us out a lot, and they dropped in for visits to make sure we were still functioning.

My friend Dick Nault, with whom I had fortuitously become instant friends just a few weeks prior to the robbery, became a great support. He invited me to stay with his parents, who lived outside of Chicago. He lived at home to save money and would drive back and forth to classes. So I did that. I lived in this Protestant home and learned, among other things, that many families do not have cocktails before dinner, which of course Irish families tend to do unless they're teetotalers, which my family was not.

Eventually, there was a trial. Sharon and I were the only ones to participate. Neither of us was there for the other's testimony. I had never been through a trial of course, so I was fascinated by the whole thing. But it was one of the hardest experiences I have ever endured.

In the end, one man got off, but three went to jail in Joliet, Illinois.

This was in the spring of 1971. My community had encouraged me to get away, so I had booked a ticket to travel to Europe in April, but the trial got postponed more than once. After it began, it went slowly, and when it was over the justice department wanted us to stay around until the sentencing took place. In those days, you were committed to an airline ticket whether your life changed or not. So I had to give up the use of my ticket. This was a big deal. My relatives in Europe were all waiting for me.

The Irish police felt so bad for me that they pooled together their money to pay for a new ticket. My friend John and some other Jesuits were going to Europe at the same time, and we arranged to meet. We spent a week in Paris and took a trip up the Alps. It was wonderful. I had not felt safe before that trip, but I felt safe there.

By the time my community allowed me to move back to Chicago to finish my studies, three months had gone by. I lost interest in the dissertation. It was tough. I was still afraid. A dear friend, Sister Columba, came down to see me. She has a temper and a sense of humor like you've never seen. She said to me, "You've got to get out of here." Then she went to the University's real estate office and said, "If you're not going to do anything to help these women, you can keep your bricks and mortar and you know where they're going to end up."

So I got an apartment in a faculty building. The university was not supposed to allow that, but a nun who had been raped and tortured got some special treatment. I got a really nice third floor apartment and, wouldn't you know, visible outside my window was the apartment of none other than the author Saul Bellow. That was great fun. He had no interest in my activities, of course, but you can be sure I was aware of his.

After things died down, I innocently wanted to visit the men who robbed us, thinking that if they saw me they would know I'm a person and not a dog. But nobody who had a car would drive me to Joliet, so I never got there. Some years later I got a letter saying that they wanted to re-try those criminals. I had moved on in my life and I didn't have the stomach for it. So they let them go free.

I don't see any lesson in this for other people except as a warning: don't be so naive about the relationships that are forming in your life.

There was one silver lining in the aftermath of this ordeal. A friend of mine at Chicago, a Jesuit priest who was an English major, offered to send my paper on *Black Like Me* to its author, John Howard Griffin. Griffin was a convert to Catholicism and had written a wonderful book on Thomas Merton. My friend included a note that said I had been injured in a racial situation and wanted to share my paper with him. He included a book of prose by Thomas Merton and asked him to inscribe it for me. John Howard Griffin read the paper and returned the book with a very nice half-page note written in the front. I was thrilled.

To be grateful is to recognize the love of God
in everything he has given us—
and he has given us everything.
Every breath we draw is a gift of his love,
every moment of existence is a grace,
for it brings with it immense graces from him.
Gratitude, therefore, takes nothing for granted,
is never unresponsive,
is constantly awakening to new wonder and praise
of the goodness of God.
For the grateful person knows that God is good,
Not by hearsay but by experience.
And that is what makes all the difference.
(Thomas Merton, Thoughts in Solitude*)*

IV

Three Weddings and a Family

After I got my Ph.D., my perspective shifted. I was no longer thinking of teaching high school, which I originally thought would be my resting place. I began to wonder if I should pursue a different way to use my education. I never resolved that, because I didn't know who had the authority to make that decision since I was living on my own, outside the religious community. Is it up to the community? Is it up to me? Who's calling the shots?

I was always thinking about God. Sometimes it was with deep affection. Sometimes it was with confusion. "I'm so puzzled," I would pray. "I don't know what you want. Would you please be more explicit?" I assumed God couldn't care less about academic stuff. But in retrospect I can see how God's hand was in all that unfolded. So much good happened without my manipulation.

When I was on the job market, I didn't know if I should look for something in sociology, or one of the other social sciences, or in education. The first job that came along was in sociology. I hadn't thought much about it and didn't know much about it—the story of my life. It turned out every job offer was in sociology.

One was from a private university in Pittsburgh. I discovered it was a science-oriented place, and I didn't think of myself as a scientist. But they offered me a job and I thought, Wow, this is getting away from me. I got an offer from a school in Florida, too, where the chair of the department had said, "So you are our Token Tit for this recruitment." Needless to say, I rejected that offer.

I had six offers in all. I didn't want to go to any of them, but knowing that I needed to have bread to eat the following year, I decided I should pick one. At the last minute, I got a call from Wisconsin inviting me to visit and apply for a job there. And I thought, Madison! It's only half a continent away from New York, and I have friends there. I was happy to accept their offer.

There I fell in with a great group of people. My cohort included a Chinese scholar, my dear friend Richard Schoenherr, a guy from Vermont, and me. We got along beautifully together. Those were good years.

They were also lonely because, while I loved my cohort, the three others were married with children, which obviously was not true of me. People looked at what I was doing—namely, getting these offers and choosing

Wisconsin—and probably thought, Six offers, what a luxury; she must be so proud.

But I wasn't feeling that. I didn't feel like I was anybody special. I didn't feel like I was going to make a good teacher because I had never taught at the college level. And what I really desired, now that I was through with my studies, was to marry and have children, to build a regular life.

So it was a lonely time, but it was a happy time, too. Teaching at the university level did something to my head. I began to think of myself as an academic, maybe somebody who actually would have a career as a scholar rather than as a super teacher or something. Wisconsin opened up avenues besides teaching that were of interest to me. I would fantasize about creating a formula for something or other. That was thrilling. Or maybe I would solve a theorem that nobody had solved before.

As it turned out, I loved being a professor. And it delighted me that I was involved in an activity that allowed participation in the life of the Holy Spirit. I think of the Holy Spirit as wisdom and I think of the communication of knowledge as part of the Spirit's work. I loved the fact that I had a profession that included God in such a direct way. I didn't take the pious practices very seriously at the time. But teaching was a spiritual gift to me and I was thrilled by it.

After two years of teaching at Wisconsin, I informed my Superior that I wanted to leave my community. It was a relief to go. It also seemed like the smart thing to do; it was the smart people who were leaving the religious life because the Church was being so difficult.

My exit was not dramatic as it would have been had I been living in the convent. There, if you chose to leave, you were smuggled out at night. When my friend Maureen left, for instance, they returned her street clothes to her and whisked her away in the dark. She was gone. Nobody talked about it; nobody wrote to her. It was as if she didn't exist.

I didn't have that kind of experience. I wrote a letter to the Provincial, the nun in charge of the local group, who responded by letter, giving me permission. I did not have to otherwise interact with her. The letter said something like "Marie Teresita Hallinan is being dispensed from her religious vows." Simple.

My parents didn't say too much about my decision to leave. My dad was supportive and said, "Maureen, anything you want to do, you can make pleasing to God." My mother, on the other hand, was very unhappy about it and offered to ask the community to take me back. I think I informed them in the same way I informed them about the robbery: I went home, told them, and left.

There isn't a specific day in my mind that I attach to my leaving. It was more like a gestalt than anything like what you read in a true story about a nun leaving the convent. It was a big deal in terms of my relationship to God. I spent the longest time as a nun trying to make sure that this decision was consistent with what God wanted of me. One of my thoughts, which I remember very distinctly, was that God wanted me to leave. I didn't regret leaving because I was convinced it was God's will for me.

After that, I knew I had to find another way to dedicate myself to God but I couldn't figure out what it could be. I joined the Newman Center and participated in that spiritual life to some degree. And I realized that, although the people that had become my community were maybe not as God-centered as I was, they were certainly sensitive, kind, and good. In them, I found the dedication to helping others. That satisfied me. My great dilemma about leaving the religious life was over.

I started dating. I went out with some characters and occasionally wondered whether it might be better to stay single. There was no one I wanted to pursue a career with, so to speak.

Then I met Art Grubert.

Art grew up in Brooklyn. He had one older sister, Jeanmarie. They were very close. Their father was an alcoholic and left the family when Art was fourteen. Art loved his father, but his father was threatening to his mother, so Art asked him to leave. It's a sad story because Art was such a tender, gentle person.

After that, Art's mother was the supporter of the family; she did administrative work of some kind. Art was so proud of her. She sang with the Carnegie Choral Society and got Art involved as a chorister. He loved that. He loved singing; he loved to perform; and he loved singing with his mother.

Art went to an all-boys Jesuit high school where he received excellent academic and religious training. He went on to St. Philips College and then entered Maryknoll, a mission organization of the Catholic Church, to become a priest. He and my brother John were in the same class at Maryknoll. They became close friends, and you don't get close to Art unless something special is going on.

After they were ordained as priests, Art and John were assigned to adjacent parishes in Korea. They created a pig co-op together and opened a school. Every three years they visited home and spent time with each other's families. So Art knew all my family except me because I was teaching in Wisconsin.

Art and I finally met when I went to New York for my sister Rita's wedding reception. She had married a divorced, Jewish, Congregationalist musician. That's a story in itself. They had to find a Catholic priest willing to marry them, which was a challenge because a good Catholic is not supposed to marry a divorced Jewish Congregationalist. It mixes God up altogether.

So Rita and her intended, Steve, asked Art to marry them, because Art never said no to anybody. Art told Rita and Steve that he would be delighted to marry them in the United Nations chapel, a nondenominational church in Manhattan. Rita had one caveat: "I don't want Mom and Pop at the wedding because they'll make a scene." So she and Steve assigned me a job: take our parents as far away from the chapel as possible for the afternoon of the wedding.

That's what I did. The day of the wedding, I drove my parents out of town, and my sister got married in the UN chapel. The witnesses were the doctor Rita worked for at Mt. Sinai hospital, and the doctor's secretary. They were the guests, too. No one else was invited because you know, if you can't trust your parents, who can you trust?

The following week, Rita and Steve had a reception. They also had a plan: they wanted to set up Art and me. They thought we would make a wonderful pair.

My parents and I were at the reception. Art was too, of course, along with many friends. It was a big party, like a block party. Several people were playing billiards in the basement, and Art asked me to play. Even though I didn't know how, we hung around together the rest of the day. Then we parted ways. I had no feelings for him at all, which was odd because I was looking for a husband. It was also frustrating to my sister and Steve; things hadn't developed between us as planned.

Then Thanksgiving rolled around, and Rita told Art that I wanted him to come to Wisconsin for the holiday. Then Rita told me that Art wanted to come to Wisconsin for Thanksgiving. They really did not know how to match-make at all. But that's what happened. Art came out for Thanksgiving with Rita and Steve and we had a very nice foursome for the weekend.

Saturday night we decided to go out dancing. Oh how I loved to dance. After an hour or so, Rita and Steve said, "We want to go home, but don't let us rush the two of you." I thought, Great, we'll dance a while longer. Then all of a sudden, I distinctly remember thinking, I'm alone with him. How did that happen? It was so obviously orchestrated.

On Sunday, Rita and Steve left, but Art stayed. That night, we lit a fire in the fireplace; it was snowing and beautiful, outside and in. We started to talk and ended up talking through the night. We got to know each other pretty well. At dawn, Art said, "By the way, what do you think of engagements?" "Oh," I said, "I guess they're okay under certain circumstances." Then the topic changed somehow.

The next morning I went to the university to teach a class. When I got home for lunch, I thought, Did Art propose to me, or what was that? So I asked a question—very cleverly worded, I thought—the gist of which was, "Did you propose to me last night? "

Art said, "Of course I did." And I said, "Oh, okay. Well, let me think about it for a little while."

He said, "You mean you have questions?" I said, "I wasn't sure if you were proposing."

He said, "Oh, I'm sorry. Yes, I was proposing." This is preposterous, but nothing in my life is simple. Of course, I said yes.

Then I had to tell my parents, who were a long way away. I decided to say that we were thinking about getting married, hoping that would keep them quiet. It did, surprisingly.

Art was living in New York City at this point, in Stuyvesant Town, on the lower end of Manhattan. We started our courtship by flying back and forth to visit each other every couple of weeks. We got to like each other a lot. He really was a wonderful person. We made it through that next year that way.

But one year of long-distance dating is enough. Art decided to join me in Madison and we agreed that he probably should have a job. These were hard to come by in Madison, which is not a large city. So Ed Bridges, a faculty member at Chicago and a good friend of mine, said he would help me get a job at Stanford University in northern California. Then Art could find work in the San Francisco area. So we drove across the country, found a place to live in the house of a friend who was going away for a time, and Art started looking for a job.

We did a lot of traveling those first few weeks. It was beautiful. Then school started and I had to teach. Art tried to get a full-time job while also selling real estate and studying to be a travel agent. He sold a house and a condo, and then he gave up because selling real estate in California at that time was fiercely competitive.

All this time, Art was still a priest. You might wonder how we could square that fact and our Catholicism with our choice to "live in sin." I did not have a problem with it, believing as I did that rules around cohabitation came more from people like my mother than they did from God. But we did want to get married.

In order to leave the priesthood and be eligible to be married, Art had to write a letter to the Pope himself. For the Pope to dispense him from his vows, Art had to admit that he was married. In other words, if you got married, then you could be dispensed from your vows. So late that summer of 1975, Art and I got married by a justice of the peace in the state supreme court in San Francisco and sent the Pope a copy of the marriage certificate. We expected the Pope would send his disposition by Christmas. And we thought, Great, we'll have this wrapped up in time to get married in the Church next fall.

The Pope was not following our time table. His answer didn't come and didn't come. But we had planned the wedding, and I had done so much thinking and worrying and wondering about how to marry Art without my parents going bananas, I wanted to go on with it. So the next fall, on September 11, 1977, we got married on 5th Avenue in New York City at Marymount Academy.

It was a lovely wedding, but Art and I knew we weren't truly married in the eyes of the Church. The two priests knew, too, though we had not told them, and they had not asked. What you don't know won't hurt you.

Lo and behold, sometime the following March, the letter from the Pope came. By this time I was five months pregnant; we were delighted we could finally be married in the eyes of the Church. So in April, Art and I, the priest, his dog, and a witness of some sort, sat in a circle of armchairs at Stanford University and we got married. That was the real marriage. I thought it tremendously amusing to have a dog and our unborn child as the witnesses to our real wedding.

I told a very few, select people this story a long time later.

During my pregnancy with our first-born, Christopher, obstetricians were just starting to use amniocentesis, and because of my age they suggested that I have that. Art and I decided we would find out the gender of the baby. A boy! The whole experience of having the amniocentesis and seeing the ultrasound was so exciting!

Christopher was such an easy baby. He was beautiful: blond, blue-eyed, the perfect size. Like his own son, Thomas, Christopher was very somulent. He sat, laughed, ate, ate some more, and played. I used to bring him to class with me. I had a big office across from the seminar room, and I would put His Majesty to bed with soft music playing, step across the hall, and teach. Art would gladly have taken the baby while I taught. But I wanted to take him. I adored this kid; I didn't want to be away from him for a minute.

Then Renee burst into the world. She cried more than Christopher because she was born with a sensory motor integration deficit; she was very sensitive to touch. She wasn't difficult in terms of not being pleasant, but she just wasn't comfortable. She couldn't help it, and I couldn't help her. But basically they were both healthy babies, with no major illnesses.

Having children expanded my world enormously and increased my happiness by great gobs. It astonished me to have these babies; I was a nun for seventeen years, for crying out loud. To have children after thinking I was never going to be married, let alone have children, was too good to be true. They were splendid years.

I have to confess that I didn't converse with God much in those days, but I was filled with an enormous gratitude for my family. Gratitude was my interaction with God. We didn't go to mass much. We would have wanted to provide that model for our family, but the Church was so conservative, and it made us so angry. Plus I couldn't stand the sexism of the clergy.

So we didn't go much, and it didn't really bother me. Being Catholic was part of who we were, and are. We didn't have to talk about it or even practice it in order for it to be true. We always thought of ourselves as Catholic. Still, that probably deserves some more reflection: a nun who stopped going to church. But there you have it.

At Stanford I taught both in the school of education and the department of sociology. They hired me in the school of education, but I found it pretty shallow. I wanted to teach in the department of sociology with the likes of Nancy Tuma, a gifted social scientist who among other things studied inequality and stratification—the way society or an organization divides itself according to rank, class, and so on. The sociology department turned me down several times and then finally said yes. That's when I jumped. It was more academic by a long shot. It was more interesting and more highly regarded.

As a mathematician, I was of a mind that to teach social science well, I had to show my students how one derives the formulas. Well, that is not the way you teach probability courses in a social science class. The university offered math so-and-so for sociologists, and sociology students didn't want to learn formulas. They hated it. But I loved formulas and I taught them, and the students learned well enough to earn passing grades, at least. Eventually I began to see where they were coming from, so I dropped the formulas, and concentrated on the outcomes. But if ever a mathematician reads this book, they will know exactly how difficult that was. The students desecrated my precious mathematics. The nerve!

Nancy Tuma and I were interested in interracial schools, interracial practices within schools, and the way these practices affected children. We got a big grant and used it to collect a data set on kids' interactions. Nancy and I published a couple of good articles based on those data, one on children's interpersonal relationships in interracial schools, and another on their relationships in single-gender schools. The momentum was starting to build on how race can influence kids' relationships and productivity, so our work got a wildly positive response.

Rich Williams was one of my students at Wisconsin. Nancy and I needed a research assistant who was quick, and that was Rich Williams. He and I later worked together on other projects; he was interested in stratification and I was interested in organization, so we tried to see how either stratification or organizations influenced students' achievement. Rich had a lot of quantitative skills that I didn't have, and I had a lot of substantive interests that he didn't have, so it was a good match. We ended up publishing some articles together.

Initially, Art and I were open to the idea of moving to Stanford permanently, but after Christopher was born and we were more familiar with the California lifestyle, we independently and together decided it was not the place we wanted to raise our children. It was hedonistic; people were not interested in forming communities.

So we went back to Wisconsin and stayed for seven more years. I moved back into the same academic scene with the same friends. Art took a job in international student affairs, where he eventually became director. He had traveled to practically every country in the world and knew many languages and cultures. He didn't like the university setting because he wasn't a scholar, and UW wanted to be known for its scholarship. They were so status-conscious in terms of academic excellence. He was very useful to Wisconsin, but he didn't feel valued there.

He worked closely with the international students, processing their applications, supervising visas and passports, and fostering community among them and their families. We were heavily involved with them socially. We had many students spend holidays with us; the faculty came over a lot, too. Often we couldn't understand each other; we grunted and bowed a lot. Very few people at Wisconsin knew about this kind of outreach, but I could see it up-close. It was really impressive.

My area of expertise became sociology of education. I studied stratification in some shape or form; when you were in the sociology department at Wisconsin, you couldn't get away with not studying stratification. My work focused on the subject from an interpersonal perspective. I looked at schools as organizations and how they functioned and, in the functioning, the influence of interpersonal connections on students. In other words, how the interaction of children with children, and children with teachers, influenced their achievement.

I decided to leave Madison when the department became weaker than it had been. The school was in a financial crunch; funds dried up and many of the strongest faculty members left. I didn't want to be the last one out. Tim O'Meara, Notre Dame's provost at the time, recruited me with an offer of an endowed chair. I couldn't pass that up, so I headed to Notre Dame and became the Hazel P. White Professor of Sociology. I was the second female endowed chair at the university.

There is no college of education at Notre Dame, and this bothered me. Then I had an idea, which involved my new acquaintance, Fr. Tim Scully. I knew of our mutual interest in education because he had started the Alliance for Catholic Education (ACE). I also knew that ACE, which gives master's degrees to its graduates, had to work through the University of Portland to make that happen—an inconvenience if there ever was one—because Notre Dame had no degree-granting program in education at the time. So one day I invited him to have lunch with me at the Morris Inn. Over our salads, I gave him my famous stare and said, "The Holy Spirit is calling you to found the Institute for Educational Initiatives at Notre Dame."

Tim looked at me like I was nuts and said, "What are you talking about? I'm a vice president in the provost's office. I don't have time for that." And I said, "I believe you are being called to form this institute." He said, "How are we going to do it?" And I said, "Let's just do it."

Providentially, not long after this I received a job offer from my friend Terry Sullivan, who was provost at the University of Texas-Austin, to become dean of the education school. Notre Dame's then-provost, Nathan Hatch, was fairly new and could not afford to lose one of the university's most senior women in the early weeks of his position. So I pulled out all the stops. I told him if he wanted me to stay, he had to create the Institute for Educational Initiatives and provide the funds for it.

That's how we got the Institute. Nathan made me director, but I always hated administration and was frankly not good at it. So after about six months, I told Tim I needed out. He stepped in as director and I created the Center for Research on Educational Opportunity (CREO) and directed that. I took the funding with me, by the way, which made the IEI something of a shell. But I knew Tim could handle that. He can raise money from a rock.

Our friendship grew over the years because we're both funny; we just enjoyed each other. I was nervy enough to say outrageous things to him, which he loved. And over time we realized that we could trust and confide in each other. It became a wonderful partnership.

At some point Tim introduced me to Michael Pressley, a brilliant researcher in psychology who served as ACE's academic director. Tim knew that Mike and I were both thick-headed, and for his own enjoyment he got us talking about our research. I promoted sociological research over psychological research, of course, and made no bones about it. The more I talked, the angrier Mike became. In turn, he started downplaying sociological research, which made me furious. He communicated to me that he thought I was dumb and there was no need, especially in ACE, for the kind of research I was doing. I retorted with a couple of zingers of my own. Our relationship was frosty for a while.

Mike was editor of a journal and he wrote a model review that he shared with several of us. It was excellent. When I read that I thought, I can't think he's so stupid if he's so smart. Also, he was brave, battling so many bouts of cancer as he did and not complaining about it, at least in my hearing. In the end, I very much admired him. He left a great legacy when he died.

What do I hope I'm remembered for as an academician? I would like to have made some contribution to our understanding of schools. I think the closest I have come to that is to make a little more clear how the structure of a school affects the way children learn.

Live in faith and hope
even though it be in darkness
since in this darkness it is God
who supports the soul.
Cast your care on God, since he has care of you.
He won't forget you.
(St. John of the Cross, Letter 20*)*

V

Healing Darkness

When I was about five months pregnant with Renee, I began to have strong contractions. We thought we were going to lose her. Art was singing at Easter Mass and I was sitting with a group of friends when the contractions started. They took me to the hospital, and I stayed there overnight for evaluations. To stop the contractions, the doctors gave me terbutaline. It had serious side effects. I started having hallucinations—saw myself floating around the moon and dancing on the clouds—but they kept giving it to me throughout the day and night.

After a while the contractions stopped and they let me go home, but they kept me on the medication. I took it for the rest of the pregnancy until two weeks before Renee was due. We saved her, but the medication had taken its toll. Before Renee was in school I knew that her learning was somehow delayed.

Renee has faced her disabilities remarkably well. There have been many obstacles for her to overcome, as you can imagine. I pushed her as far as possible to live up to her abilities. She took double English and double math classes, downhill skiing, dancing, photography, horseback riding. Renee loved extracurricular activities. Every time some new opportunity came up, Art would say, "Don't push her to do that." But I would and she would end up loving it.

When you have a child with a disability, you really need to advocate on his or her behalf. And you have to be tough, which I am. I fought for her rights. PennySaver, for example, is a free advertising paper that had drawing contests for children—unless they were disabled, in which case they were not allowed to participate. So I went down there and challenged that rule. When they refused to change it, I said, "Then create a contest for kids who have disabilities." They did, and guess who won? Renee. We hung that one on the wall. There are a million stories like that.

Renee has always been a good reader, but math was a challenge. I asked to sit in her math classes, and did that for a few years to help her. So she learned some math. We got her to the point where she could use a calculator to calculate a tip, and so on. Just this year she planned and took a vacation by herself. These things mean so much. People are quick to assume that someone with a disability is not educable. Renee is educable. She uses learned information in the real world.

After she graduated from high school, I thought, What do we do next? I figured she would never be able to get a job without at least an associate's degree, so she enrolled in a program at Holy Cross College, which was a two-year college at the time, and did well. But she couldn't pass the math exam. So I went over to talk to the president and said, "You know, you should have special classes for people who have special needs." It took a lot of talking and arguing, but finally they agreed to give her a special class in math. And lo and behold, she passed. She transferred to Indiana University-South Bend to finish her degree, an associate's in general education.

Then Holy Cross College became a four-year institution. Renee applied to complete the next two years, and she was rejected. I went marching in again and asked the president, "Why did you reject my daughter?" He explained that there was some new study abroad requirement for students, and he argued that her special needs meant they could not adequately protect her if she studied abroad. So Holy Cross was out.

Goshen College had a special education program, so Renee enrolled there. She spent almost a full year there, but the program was hopeless. I didn't think it was a healthy place for her to be. It sounded like they merely tolerated the special ed kids and weren't providing them with a life-giving atmosphere. Finally, Renee transferred to a regular program at Ivy Tech, and she passed. She earned a second associate's degree in early childhood education. I was so proud of her.

✝ ✝ ✝

Art never accepted Renee's disability. I couldn't talk about it with him; he didn't believe it. He didn't believe he had Huntington's disease, either. Neither one of us did at first.

He had been acting very strangely at home. One night, we had a party with about twenty guests. The liquor was flowing and people were happy, laughing, having fun. Art had just come back from Egypt and had bought clothes there. During the party, he put on one of his new tunics. Then he proceeded to stand on the piano chair and sing a song, which is all well and good. But he wouldn't come down. I persuaded him eventually, but it was so embarrassing. What can you do?

Then he began acting crazier—I say that word flippantly. Why? Out of anger? Maybe; they were tough years. When I say crazy, I don't mean violent. He was a gentle, kind man. He became stubborn. He said and did nonsensical things. For instance, one winter weekend we were taking a long walk together on Michigan Ave., and he insisted on walking in the middle of the street. He left me and went farther into the street and started walking faster in front of me. There was a couple on the corner, and the woman said to me, "Excuse me but I think that man needs help." I said, "Don't worry. He's my husband; I'm keeping an eye on him." But that struck me. I thought, How does Art not understand that he's attracting people's attention?

I was frightened. What if I couldn't take care of him? What was I going to do? Every time we went out for a walk that winter, I was afraid that he would leave me and I wouldn't be able to get him back.

Art and I both had cars then. One day we passed each other on Angela Street, a busy road just south of campus. He stopped in the middle of the street to say hi. I said, "We should pull over." But he wouldn't, even in the middle of Angela Street. After that incident, we had our first of many talks about public behavior. He did not want to admit there was anything wrong, which I later learned is a symptom of Huntington's. Slowly it began to sink into my thick skull that we were going to have to make some changes in our family and it was up to me to make them.

I did not know it was Huntington's at this point. I was afraid of Alzheimer's. I brought him to a neurologist, who tested him for a series of diseases that have these same symptoms. Art kept resisting: there was nothing wrong with him; he didn't need any testing; blah blah blah.

The day we got Art's final results was hellish. The doctor said, "I have good news and bad news." Don't you hate it when they say that? "The good news is, you don't have Alzheimer's." I thought, Great! Game over. That's what I was concerned about. But Art kept sitting there as if he had an intuition that something else was brewing.

"You do have something that could lead to dementia," the doctor went on to say. "The bad news is . . ." and he paused to be dramatic. "You have Huntington's disease." Art and I didn't say anything because neither of us had ever heard of Huntington's disease. The doctor explained that it is a disease that affects your cognitive and physical functioning. I said, "Can we do anything about it?" The doctor replied that we could do various things to minimize the impact. I was thinking, Is it fatal? As he outlined the disease, I couldn't absorb anything else.

Art said, "I don't have this." We left the office and I said, "Let's sit here for a minute in the waiting room." Art was stunned. He didn't say much, like he was overpowered by some evil force. I started to cry, and Art kept saying, "How do they know? How do they know?" He was a mass of confusion and fear.

We went home and I got everything out of the library that I could find on Huntington's disease. I read Merck's manual from beginning to end; I read autobiographies again and again, hungry to learn. It was very hard to get information. I brought stuff to Art to read, but quickly realized that he was not accepting it. He was not reading anything.

I talked to the doctor again, trying to find solutions in my typical way. "Tell us what to do; whatever it takes," I told him. The doctor kept saying, "No, you don't treat Huntington's that way. You learn all that you can about it. There are many questions, but very few answers."

I wasn't sure what to do or how to integrate the children's lives into this new life. It's funny. It's the same thing I'm experiencing now. The unknowing. What's going to happen to us? How can I prepare? How can I prepare the children? How can we keep the children's lives on an even keel? The truth is, I did not prepare the children well. You might think that's strange, since these questions were always going through my head. But the children will tell you that I am not a nurturing person. I should have talked to them about all of this. But I didn't.

My hair lost several shades of red during those years. They were tough. The toughest part was not having Art as a real partner in the process. He never mentioned that he felt Renee was disabled in any way. And he didn't talk about his Huntington's disease. And you know, when someone stops talking about something, you stop talking to them about it. It doesn't make for much of a marriage.

✝ ✝ ✝

In December of 2006, I woke up in the middle of the night, and I guess I got up, though I'm not sure why. I wasn't in pain. But I knew something was wrong. Art was in assisted living by this point, so I started to walk from my bedroom to call for Renee. It began to dawn on me that I had had a stroke because I couldn't talk, and I couldn't walk very well. Renee took me directly to the ER at Memorial Hospital.

The whole thing was unbelievable. Even in the wake of the stroke, I was aware of how preposterous it was. I wanted to say to the admitting nurse, "Hi my name is Clarabelle and I live in a shoe." They put me in a bed and left me there for what felt like several months. I'm sure they put a priority mail sign above my bed—get this woman out of here. Finally they let me move around a little bit. The first thing they asked is if I had had any lunch. I thought, Can you please deal with the stroke first, and we can deal with lunch later?

I could hardly speak; several doctors came out during the day and did different tests with big machines. I asked if they could tell me anything. They told me I had suffered a stroke, that one side of my body was probably damaged more seriously than the other, and that I would probably never be restored to my normal self. I felt like saying, "How do you know what my normal self is? How dare you make that assumption?"

It was a couple of days before Christmas, so they offered to either hurry things up so I could go home, or to keep me over the holiday so they could do more tests and determine what damage had been done. I wanted to ask, "What brought it on?" My voice was so weak, though, and the doctors didn't tell me anything. I decided to stay in the hospital for Christmas. I spent two weeks there. It was so boring. Slowly I began to improve, but never to the point I hoped for.

Before the stroke, I was very physically active. I swam every day at 5:30 am, including weekends, though then I got a break because the pool didn't open until 7:00 am. I worked every day and never took a day off. On campus, I walked the ten flights of stairs to my office in Flanner Hall and never took the elevator. I did not rest much.

After the stroke, I pushed myself to get stronger. I had every kind of physical and occupational therapy known to man. But to this day I need much more rest. I have lost a lot of weight because swallowing is hard. And my voice is still weak.

Adding insult to injury, a few years ago I was diagnosed with Parkinsonism. If someone else in our family had to be diagnosed with a disease, I suppose it was my turn. But it took a while for the truth to sink in.

Parkinsonism.

Such a strange name. I remember well when I was diagnosed. And I remember where I was when I finally accepted it. I was on the South Shore Train.

I had been suffering symptoms that I thought were related to my stroke—problems walking and swallowing and back trouble. My doctor in South Bend suspected something else was going on and suggested I get evaluated in Chicago. I thought to myself, This is not true. I simply do not have a disease. Don't they see that I don't? But I submitted myself to testing. On the first trip, I was very grumpy; how dare they tell me I have a disease I don't have? On the train coming home, I was overwhelmed with emotion. How can this be, that Art has Huntington's and I have some neurological disease? God doesn't do that. God does not do that.

My doctor in South Bend sent me back to Chicago to see a specialist. Christopher met me at the train; he was a good support. He was living in Washington, DC, but he flew over so many times to accompany me to appointments, talk to the doctors—both in Chicago, and at the Cleveland Clinic.

The specialist I was assigned to did not impress me at all. As soon as I saw him, I thought, Right. You are a specialist? Bull. You don't act like one. It requires certain kinds of behavior, which you do not exhibit. During the exam, he put his hands on my face and said he was so glad I had come. I don't like to be touched, especially by doctors who are supposed to be specialists in rare diseases. I never went back to him.

Eventually Parkinsonism was the diagnosis I was given. On the way home from that visit, I remember thinking, This family is going to fall apart. That's when it started to sink in. What is going to happen to us? It was such a real question. I don't know. I still don't know.

I have not had many questions for God about all this. Even as recently as this morning, as I walked the halls talking to God, I said, "You must have given me this disease." God often stops talking when I get grumpy like this; I think he or she has thin skin. But maybe what God intends to say is, "You have Parkinsonism; I'm aware of that. I know about Art's Huntington's disease. I know about all of that. And I expect you to deal with it as well as a human being can deal with it."

To that, I reply, "I don't know what you expect from me, and I'm doing the best I can. Could you give me some hints please? I want to respond to it in the way I think you would respond in a similar situation." There is always silence on the other end of the line.

Art was not around for my diagnosis because he was living at Holy Cross, where I am now. During that time Renee and I saw him a lot because he lived so close. As his illness progressed, he moved into advanced levels of care here and then finally to a facility in western Indiana, called Summerfield. It was a frumpy little place.

The last birthday he was alive, Renee and I went down to see him. I said, "Hi sweetheart, do you know what day it is?" And he said, "Of course! It's my birthday!" Those were such wonderful words to me. He always knew us and looked visibly happy to see us.

The evening of May 4, 2010, Renee and I were in the kitchen when the phone rang. I answered it. "This is Patty from Summerfield," said the voice on the other end of the line. "I just wanted to tell you that it's 7:20 pm here now, and your husband just passed." And I said, "Well, where was he going?" And she said, "I don't know." "Well," I said, "I don't understand. Did he get sick or something?" And she said, "No, he died." I mean, we're from Queens. We don't say "passed."

Since my voice is so weak, I put Renee on the phone to call our relatives. She spent about two hours talking to people; she carried it off beautifully in the midst of sorrow and despair. I was so pleased, and I knew Art would be, too.

Initially, I had some strange thoughts. I started wondering, Is he lying down? Is he stiff? Then I began to think about how to proceed. I was frightened. I had no experience with this. Where did his body need to be, and how would I get it there? Should I send it to New York? Should I send it to South Bend? What about cremation? Does he need a new suit? I called Tim Scully and said, "Art just died and I have no idea what to do." Tim thought for a minute and said, "Don't worry about a thing." His mother had died not long before this, and her funeral was lovely. He asked, "Would you like me to repeat my mother's funeral?" I said, "Sure." Then he said again, "Don't worry about a thing."

The next morning, Tim called. "Everything is all set," he said. I asked him, "Where is Art now?" Tim said, "He's in the funeral home in South Bend, where my mother was." I was astonished at the speed with which that was done.

That afternoon Renee and I went to the funeral home. The director kept asking me questions that I didn't know the answers to. All I wanted to do was see Art. Finally, they let me into the funeral parlor to see him, which I thought was mighty fine of them. My husband, right? It struck me, to see his body the first time. "This is what it's like," I said to myself. "I always wondered what it was going to be like, seeing my husband dead." And there it was. There's something about death in general and funerals in particular that is unreal. Because you sort of take it for granted, the validity of the experience you're going through, even as you're functioning on a level apart from that experience.

We chose a plot in the Cedar Grove cemetery. It's a nice spot. There's a tree. When we bought it, the undertaker asked, "Who's going to be buried here?" "Myself, my husband, and my daughter," I said. He asked, "Now, am I correct in thinking that Arthur goes in the middle and you go on one side, and Renee goes on the other?" I said, "Oh no, that's not the way we lived our lives. I will go in the middle." Feminist. It doesn't matter, but it was funny because he was so shocked. It happened again when they gave us the mortuary cards. I was to pick out the ones I wanted for the wake, but after shuffling through them I said, "None of these will be useful to us. These are very sexist and I don't want my husband's mortuary card to be sexist." So I created my own.

The funeral mass was beautiful. Tim said it, and they had gotten some people from the Notre Dame folk choir to sing, which was lovely. Tim did everything behind the scenes, and that made it a lot easier for me. Chris gave the eulogy, and Renee did a reading. I was worried about Renee and how she would get through that. But she got up and gave her thing and did fine. Tim somehow knew that I was going to worry about Renee, and when she sat down Tim gave her a big wink.

I remember looking around, seeing who was there and thinking about what I should say to them. I was very aware of my role as a mother in this event. I mean, I was worried about how Renee was taking it and how Christopher was taking it. I remember waiting to be overwhelmed with a feeling of relief that this terrible ordeal of Huntington's was over for us. The experience was staggering. I didn't feel that relief then; it came upon me after the burial. But I had no idea what was going to emerge. In the end I just sort of let it be because I didn't want to manipulate anything. This had a life of its own.

We had a lovely luncheon after the funeral. Later on, Tim and I were tallying up the bills. I said, "I don't see the bill for the luncheon." Tim said, "Somebody paid for the luncheon." I asked him who it was. "I don't know," he said, "it wasn't me." Later on I asked my brother Tom, "Do you know who paid this bill?" And he said, "Don't worry about it." Tom had done it. I thought that was very dear of him.

Renee and I used to visit the cemetery often. Those days were a rather peaceful time for us. There was a lot of relief in our feelings, relief that much of our suffering was over. Did all of that lead to conversations about death and dying? No, not really. There were instances like Tim's wink that said everything will be all right, you did fine. I had the sense that things were right on target.

✝ ✝ ✝

It is difficult for me to say where I put this suffering in my thinking about God.

I find suffering so abhorrent, so unacceptable from any perspective that I cannot think about it. Some years ago, for instance, I reached the point when I could no longer go to Good Friday services. I just had to shelve it because I could not, cannot, make any sense of it. This makes me feel like a hypocrite, because I have learned what the saints say about suffering. They have made sense of it. But I can't even think about it. When reading about the saints and their lives, I speed-read through the parts that address suffering. It's true. I can't look at suffering, even my own. I have no rational or emotional framework for it.

I feel very deeply for other people who are suffering. When I was six, we lived across the street from Mrs. Hackman, who had severe arthritis and other ailments she didn't talk about. She was an invalid. And my mother, with her Irish sense of service to others, would visit Mrs. Hackman as often as she could. She would invite me to go with her, and I thought, This must be a holy thing to do, so I will go with her because then I'll be holy, too.

I grew to like Mrs. Hackman. She was kind; she didn't complain. But I felt terrible for her because she was so crippled. After visiting I would go into my room and cry and cry and cry. This was not my style—to cry quietly. Typically, I wanted people to know when I was upset. I could be very manipulative that way. But this was different. Mrs. Hackman was suffering.

That relationship spurred me to wonder about what suffering is all about and why God allows it and whether it has anything to do with death and what happens after death.

I remember when my dad's mother died. She lived in Ireland, and of course we didn't have the technology then that we have now. So my dad learned about her death through a letter that he got in the mail. I came home from school that day, and I thought, This is terrible; my father must be suffering so much because he lost his mother, and he didn't even know until he got the letter in the mail. I carry the memory of this, of feeling so sad. And of wondering what God has to do with death and sadness.

In high school we were encouraged to engage in some sort of service activity. So I went to an orphanage. That was another sad experience. These children lived there for such a long time. I had no knowledge of a family adopting one of them, no reason to have hope for them about their futures. After a short while I stopped going. It was too painful.

Then I entered the convent and went through the period of training during which we were required to go to every funeral mass held at Marymount. It was a big place, so there were a lot of funeral masses. Going to these masses made me think about suffering, but I didn't feel the sadness. All kinds of people died, but the masses were pretty much the same.

It's different when someone you know suffers or dies, especially if you know them well; that makes suffering and death more graphic, more real. When each of my parents died, I had an overwhelming feeling of sadness, not a lack of faith; I did believe to the best of my ability that there was life after death and my parents were continuing to live in some other way. I thought, This is the point at which Mom met God and Pop met God.

My own suffering—it is what it is, or it's something God ordained. That is as much as I think about it. John of the Cross says these are things God does to draw us close to him or her. "Well," I reply, "God never asked me if I wanted to be close to him or her." And yet I am drawn to God, very strongly. My prayer is still, "God, where are you? What are you about? What is this mystery about?"

Life is this simple:
We are living in a world that is absolutely transparent
and the divine is shining through it all the time.
This is not just a nice story or a fable, it is true.
(Thomas Merton, Life Free From Care*)*

VI
Divine Shining

In 2011, Christopher married Carrie. They had a destination wedding in St. Thomas. Christopher was concerned about me because he knew it would be hard for me to travel, so he and Carrie made a reconnaissance mission to the island before the wedding to be sure I could get around without trouble.

I didn't have a dress to wear. At first I thought I did. I had had a really lovely peach dress and jacket that I wore years before to give the presidential address at ASA. The night I was packing to leave, I got that dress out to iron it and noticed that it had a stain on the front. I decided I better get rid of that stain, so I started rubbing it with a rag. Well, that was not the right thing to do. Now the pretty peach dress had a very large spot in the front, making it irrelevant to the event, because you don't wear a stained dress to your only begotten son's wedding.

The next day on the way to the wedding, I went into the dress shop at the airport and I said to the lady, "You must help me. I need a dress to wear at my son's wedding, which is tomorrow." She said, "We've had this before. I have just the thing, and it's on sale." It was the only thing available, and it was one size fits all. It looked like a multi-colored sack. It defied size. But it worked. I was set.

Carrie helped Renee pick out a dress; Carrie has wonderful taste. Uncle Dick Nault attended. He has provided so much love for our family. Dick is Renee's godfather. He has driven from his home in Ohio to South Bend many, many times to be with her, or with me if something's happening, and to spend time with Christopher. Dick is a good, good man. He didn't like my dress for the wedding, but I didn't think much of his shirt, either.

In 2013, Christopher and Carrie had their son, Thomas. I'll never in my life forget the expression on Christopher's face when he brought Thomas from the delivery room to show us. He is such a source of joy. I have said the prayers of deepest gratitude relative to Thomas, compared to anybody or anything else. How does one thank God appropriately? What does it mean to thank God? That is another question that cannot really be answered.

What am I thanking God for? For the happiest experience of life that anyone can have—that is life par excellence, to see this creature, who is just beginning to understand happenings, people, himself. Why does he chew his finger all the time? Why does he bite his toe? He has six teeth already. Doesn't that hurt?

Thomas is an easy-going baby; very playful. He could nap for days. And he is so gorgeous. I end up saying, "Thanks, God, for the best gift you could ever think of to give our family."

My friends from the old neighborhood came by this morning. "How do you like it here?" they asked. "What's it like?"

"Well," I said, "I didn't expect it to be so, how shall we say, interpersonal."

I had a boyfriend in the early weeks after I got here, a former school superintendent. Very sharp, very interesting. We went to dances here together, and to lunch at Fernwood Gardens in Niles, Michigan. We enjoyed each other's company enormously. I brought my *New York Times* to him every day until he told me he isn't a Democrat. Turns out he's a Protestant, too. You can't have everything. About a month ago, he went back to his home. His children wanted him to stay at Holy Cross, but he just couldn't stand it here anymore. I wish he would come back, but I know his children take wonderful care of him at home.

There are other suitors waiting in the wings. Another man stopped by my breakfast table recently to tell me I was very special to him. Imagine that! But he said he did not want the other residents to associate us with each other, so he suggested we meet on Sundays at the donut table and take our donuts outside to the courtyard. So now we have our donut dates.

Then there's the one who catches up with me as I walk the halls. He likes to stroke my neck, which I do not care for. Worse, he once kissed me in the middle of the dining hall. I had to break up with that one.

There are a lot of characters here—good, kind, and unusual. On my way to breakfast this morning, I said to God, "Wow, this? Yikes. Did you ever waver?" I have such half-baked answers to these questions. I don't know what God wants or planned. But here we go again: I believe, I trust that this God is deeply loving. He or she would have to be loving to create all these kinds of creatures. We humans are a weird bunch. What, was he or she really bored? Wouldn't you come up with something extraordinary if you were bored?

The people here are certainly extraordinary. And extraordinarily old. If you listen to them at breakfast—

and you really don't have any choice but to listen—you hear their woes. They say they didn't expect to be this feeble at this point in their lives; that it's a bummer to be limited and not be able to do the things they want to do. Some of what they say is holy: "I wanted to do so many things in my life but apparently God is arranging it otherwise." But to say, "I'm so sick of this wart on my toe that I can't take it any longer," that doesn't sound very holy to me.

They seem to want to be holy, and I respect them for that. Many of the brothers are wonderful. One of the priests here is the closest thing we have to Thomas Merton. He laughs. He is so utterly sincere. I'm going to have him over some day to talk about spirituality.

Most days I go to mass. Sometimes I take a book with me—Kathleen Norris or Thomas Merton—in case the homily gets too long. If I get there early, I see the pious ones, kneeling and saying the rosary. If I stay afterwards, there's another group doing the same thing. I'm not one of them; I don't like the rosary. Can you picture God on the throne listening to the same things repeated fifty or 150 times over? I feel guilty about this, though. The other day I saw some rosary beads, and I thought I heard them sneer at me: "Nah nah nah." I suspect full well that God knows what evil lies in the heart of man.

People who are holy have a keener awareness of God and God's love than I have. My faith is not strong. Sometimes, somewhere in my ego or heart I have the conviction that I am doing something that pleases this God whom I so appreciate, but the truth is I don't do anything to increase my relationship with God. It's not anything to brag about to say, "Hello, God, thank you for my friends, for my family, for this day." To have to so deliberately make myself pray in this way seems to devalue that prayer.

I really did think when I came here that I would quickly pick up a God-orientation that would make God a center of my life. I was convinced that would happen, but guess what? It hasn't, not even a little bit. This stark honesty makes me sound like a pagan. However, I have less fear about this than I did previously. Perhaps one reason is because I am in a setting with people who are seriously religious. They are kind to each other, aware of each other's disabilities and problems and illnesses, and they have chosen this religious facility as an end-of-life home, so to speak. This community gives me courage to believe that someday I will indeed be able to enter into a reflective and God-oriented frame of mind. That's what I want for the last phase of my life.

I am grateful for Truth—capital "T" Truth. Nothing is as important to me as that because God is Truth. To me Truth is reality and reality incorporates that God. Therefore reality is utterly important. If we're less than completely honest about reality, we are losing touch with God. That's what I don't want to do. And so I search for and long for reality.

Scripture is God-given Truth. You come across contradictions, but maybe they're not contradictions at all. Maybe they are levels that are deeper than we understand. If we embrace that Truth, we're embracing God. I've thought about this a long time, and I keep coming back to the same sentence or two, namely, that if we're searching for God and we embrace Truth, then we've obtained God. And that's what we want. So we really should be searching for Truth.

When I think of Truth as an image, I think of a book. A book, whatever it is, brings me such joy, such a sense of reality. This is what *is*. My friend Sonia Gernes, a now-retired English professor, poet, and author from Notre Dame, loaned me a novel not long ago called *People of the Book* by Geraldine Brooks. Its message is that every book is more than the book as we think of it. A certain perspective exists in the author's mind, and as others read it, it becomes part of their minds and experiences. The book takes on a life of its own, a history of its own. It's a wonderful insight.

Christianity is a great story. If there's a God, Christianity describes the kind of God I want him or her to be—compassionate, forgiving, all-loving. When we were in school we were taught that God is omnipotent, all-everything-good. So take any characteristic, like love, and God is all love. God is not not-love. God is all love. God is also all Truth.

In truth, I'm afraid of God the Father. I'm not afraid of the second person of God, Jesus, whom we've come to know is all-loving. We've seen what he is in a person. In Jesus, we can understand relationships. We can understand suffering. We can understand aspirations, goals. I am afraid of the fatherhood of God because I have such an inappropriate sense of who God the Father is—what he is, what he's about, what he's doing. So usually I just dismiss God the Father. He's too everything for me. I'm just a creature, but he's God.

As for the third person of the Holy Trinity, the Holy Spirit, we don't have much to go by in the Scriptures. We know the Holy Spirit came on Pentecost with a big blast of wind. I can understand what wind is, but I don't understand the holiness of wind. He talks in many languages. He knows full well that I only know one. So what is his point? But somehow I'm crazy about him. He is the Spirit of Truth, speaking and teaching us the truth so that we can resemble him. To be Truth—can you imagine that?

Seek God always as one hidden.
You honor God greatly and indeed come near to him
when you hold him to be nobler and deeper
than anything you can attain. . . .
So you do well at all times, whether life, or faith,
is smooth, or hard,
you do well to hold God as hidden,
and so to cry out to him,
"Where have you hidden?"
(*St. John of the Cross,* A Spiritual Canticle
of the Soul*)*

VII
Ending, August 2013

It seems to me that, as a religious community here, we can help each other finish this life well. Because why else are we here? We need assisted living, of course. I'm here because I can't manage by myself. But more than that, we need help keeping the body and mind alive so that we can do something else before we die.

I think my final task is to help people feel good about themselves. That means being nice to them. It's a challenge for me, because I don't like some of them and I don't like being nice to them. I don't think I'm generous enough to do it. Partly I don't want to. Partly I don't know how to do it well. It's much more rewarding to write a paper and get it published than to interact with some of these creatures. So this is a big deal, to keep this as a goal.

I think of certain friends for inspiration, like my colleague, Mark Berends. Of the many things I could say about him, one is that he always gives people the time they seem to need. He listens. That is a gift. Then there's my friend Sue; we were in the convent together. She serves with such determination and willpower. She is so generous and kind. And I wonder how she does that. I don't have one-tenth of what she has, but I want to be like her.

Last night I got up at about 3 a.m. and headed to the dining room. I have been doing that more lately, getting up multiple times in the middle of the night and walking to breakfast. I have lost the concept of time. Numbers no longer make sense to the mathematician. Parkinsonism is a cruel disease.

The night nurse lectured me about making her job more difficult because she had to attend to me in the wee hours. When I left her, I burst out crying. Why? I am not quick to cry. But she hurt my feelings. The experience made me feel like an inadequate person, a bother, who will probably spend the rest of her life doing these same things. Prowling the halls in the wee hours of the night. Shuffling to the dining room when it's not mealtime. That is depressing.

I have been falling more. The floor is cold and hard; sometimes I have to stay there a long time before I can pull myself over to the emergency cord to call for help. I am constantly bruised. My friend says, "You are at war with your body," and she's right. I don't know how much longer I can do this.

I am not feeling well these days, and I know I'm failing. But I don't know what I'm failing to. The doctors don't know or don't want to tell me. When I hit that level, whatever it is, that's when I know, this is the end. It might take a month or two or a year, but it's close. You realize that and you think, Yikes. Impossible. I wasn't supposed to get here. But here I am.

When I first got here I thought, I will probably die here. And I will probably die alone. It's a very strange idea to face.

Death is a tricky and most difficult thing. There could be nothing more profound to the human being than to be confronted with the idea of not existing, or if you're going to continue to exist, not having the foggiest idea what it's going to be like. Who's going to be there? What will we do?

Sometimes people seem cocksure of there being an afterlife and its being a wonderful one. Some think we experience ecstasy and that's all we need to experience. I don't even know what ecstasy means. I find it surprising that we don't know more about the process of death and what happens after death. Why does God want that to remain a mystery?

But if we ask to know more, it seems that we're not trusting God. If we believe that God loves us and wants us to be with him or her forever, then we won't need all the answers. And we won't be afraid of death.

I've searched for information about death in the Bible, but I don't find much that appears to be nourishing. When Art died, Tim asked me what readings I would like to have, and I said, "The Gospel of John, and the story of Lazarus dying." That's the only place where Jesus speaks of death and the afterlife so explicitly. "Take off the grave clothes," he says, and then the onlookers say, "He stinketh." I like that very much, because it confronts death face-to-face.

I wish people spoke more about it and said what they thought, what they believed, because that would strengthen us all in our faith I think. It's such a treasure to have someone you can speak to freely about death and our conception of it.

My brother Tom and I talked about death after his wife, Mila, died. They had been married for many years, and she got sick and sicker from some kind of infection, until there was no hope. In two weeks' time, she went from health to death. She was older than Tom by nine years. She had been married previously and had three wonderful boys. Mila and Tom never had children of their own because he was afraid of Agent Orange. She was the love of his life.

After Mila died, Tom and I talked often. Our sister Rita was also very faithful to him. It was a terrible time. Tom's love for Mila gave him strength to believe that good things happen after death. We would talk about God and death and people that went before us, a lot of stuff, and I felt very close to him.

We all have fantasies about dying and death. I still have to pull back every so often and say, "How does God want this scenario to play out—my death, your death?" I desperately want insight into this. What happens after we die? Who am I going to hang around with? Where am I going to get a sense of community and companionship? From other people who are dead? From total envelopment in God? These are such important questions to me.

There are stories that seem to give answers: people who have "died" and then come back, who speak of the warmth and light and goodness they experience. I don't take much comfort from those stories, though. Because I'm a scientist, I need more evidence than that. But then I think, What do I know?

I'm struck with how much elderly people think about death, and the spin they put on it. It's not as fearful to

them as I thought it might be; at least they don't show
that fear. One lady talks about suffering and death all
the time. But there does not seem to be fear in it. "This
is the way we go," she says, without questioning it. That's
the way the brothers sound, too.

I keep thinking of my friend Judith who died last year.
After she died, I thought, I have to understand this. She
was my very best friend. I could entrust anything to her.

Judy and I met in Chicago. Her husband, Richard, was
a sociology student at the university, which was how I
got to know him and how I met her. Richard had been a
Catholic priest from Detroit and Judy was in a religious
order. They met, and as so often happens: priest meets
nun, priest loves nun, and priest and nun make a life
together once they straighten out the mess with the
Church. They probably have some of the happiest
marriages I have ever seen.

Judy was so funny, so genuine, a really wonderful person.
She and Richard had two children, Andrew and Maria,
and then they adopted Joey, a child from Chicago. They
asked me if I would be his godmother. I was honored.
Joey is a treasure.

The day he was to come home they asked me to stay
with the other two children. When they walked in the
door with the new baby, Andrew was crying his heart

out. I could not comfort him. Judy quickly figured out why. She asked me, "How long ago did you change his diaper?" Then she carted him away, and he stopped crying instantly. Judy said, "Maureen, when you changed him, you left the safety pin open. It was sticking in his leg." Poor Andrew. I was not much of a babysitter.

Judy and I continued to be friends throughout the years. She was diagnosed with cancer about five years ago. I didn't see her much because we lived in different cities, but we talked almost every day. I treasured that. Judy was so good without trying to be good. She was so honest about her own death.

The day before she died she called me and said, "It's time for me now, Maureen." And I said, "I'll miss you terribly, Judy." And she said, "You'll have much love surrounding you." I said, "I've never had a friend like you." And she said, "You'll always have me as a friend." That's the kind of gorgeous stuff that she would say. That same day she said, "Dying is very hard." I keep looking to Judy for hints. She was so wise.

Maybe when the chips are down I'll think, I can't take it. Judy used to say that. She would say, "I don't know what I'm capable of believing." Or, "I don't know how I can live here." Or, "I don't know how I can live a religious life." But somehow, as my mind has gotten slow, it just seems all right that God chose to do it this way. At the same time, it hurts so badly.

Every time death happens here at Holy Cross—and it happens a lot—it is rather jolting. The way the community reacts is fascinating to me. So many people don't question death. I've assumed that means they're afraid of death. But they have told me that they are not afraid of death. So why don't they talk about it? They love to talk about their lives, but not about their death. Those who have died are "there." They know what the afterlife is. Maybe they were right and maybe they weren't right; I want to discuss this. I want to get my hands around the neck of death.

I remember a visit with my father when Art and I were living in California. My father and I went out to lunch at a place overlooking the San Francisco Bay. We were talking about all sorts of things, and I said, "Pop, do you think there's a heaven?" And he said, "I certainly hope so."

That's as stark an answer as you can get. Honest. It generates thoughts about the death/life process. I was so proud of him to be so honest, so centered, so wrapped up in spirituality and goodness. I had exactly the kind of father I would want to have. This person I adored believed all I thought were the right things to believe. That there is a God, that God loves us, that there is a life after death.

I don't care about my funeral. My death is going to come sometime. That's the "then" I care about. I care that I die peacefully and that the children are as prepared as they can be. I have a lot of confidence in Christopher's strength and Renee's resilience. They've got a lot going for them, and they've been through a lot. I am very proud of the two of them.

So here I am, seventy-three years old, in an assisted living facility that's close enough for me to be able to supervise my disabled daughter if she needs it, with a son and a grandson to whom I want to be available for as long as I can. Where do I put God in that picture? I do not know. Did God do this? Did God permit this? Does God want this? I do not know, and I do not understand people who think they do. But I will not dispose of a loving image of God. There's nothing to replace it with. I believe it. I trust it. That's all I can do.

Maureen Hallinan died peacefully just
after midnight on January 28, 2014.

Afterword

Jacob wrestles all night long. All night long, he thrashes about with an unnamed angel of the Lord, and refuses to give in. And before the struggle is over, before daybreak, before ultimately he must succumb to the sheer power of the divine challenger, he demands the angel impart a blessing upon him. The blessing is ultimately bestowed upon him after that long and utterly exhausting night at Penuel, but Jacob emerges from the encounter with a limp. A limp he will carry for the rest of his life, on his long journey through dangerous deserts and over treacherous mountains to the Promised Land.

When I reflect upon the life of the remarkable woman we remember and celebrate in this spiritual memoir, I cannot help but call to mind that story from Hebrew scripture. Maureen wrestled with that same angel—all night long. She tossed and turned and thrashed about, but she *never* gave in. That angel found out something as he wrestled with this deeply intelligent, hilarious, tenacious, determined, insightful, undaunted, courageous woman: This is one stubborn lady! And as she moved through her remarkably full life as a breathtakingly successful and stunningly brilliant scholar, teacher, and intellectual, you could see in Maureen a deepening holiness. Little by little, you could see in this truculent woman a quiet mellowing, a generous surrender. Though perhaps limping a bit through the journey, as anyone does who engages with equal ferocity the very presence of God, Maureen came to embody for us what it means to be utterly faithful.

So many, many memories. How could anyone ever forget Maureen? I remember our very first encounter, nearly twenty-five years ago. I was giving a lecture in the Hesburgh Center for International Studies at the University of Notre Dame, on the vocation of a Catholic university. And there sat this lady near the front of the audience, simply *glaring* at me, evincing a mixture of what appeared to me to be disapproval and pity. Though I didn't know who she was, I was simply terrified of her. I sought her out at the reception after my talk, and introduced myself, and she made it clear that she had little time for a white, male, chauvinistic priest such as myself.

I found her at once scary and intriguing. I invited her to lunch, and there, one-on-one, I discovered one of the most marvelous people I would ever meet in my life. Someone who would become a treasured soulmate and one of my life's great friends.

Maureen simply refused to let you off the hook. She wasn't one for trivialities or idle chatter. She had no time for it, and if you weren't being totally honest with her about something important in your life, she would just chew you out. She possessed this remarkably sophisticated BS detector. And being Irish myself, most of our kind like to embellish and dissimulate, and employ humor to blunt the sometimes painful truth. We almost never want to get to the heart of the matter. Well, if you tried that with Maureen, you were toast!

Maureen was simply uncompromising, not just in terms of her intellectual standards, which were formidable, but in terms of everything. (She did not suffer fools gladly, which is one reason why our friendship always struck me as the one exception she made to that rule!)

This same stubbornness reached into every corner of her life, especially her relationship with God and the Catholic Church. Remember that remarkable story from the sixth chapter of John's Gospel, from the very end of the "Bread of Life" discourses? What a great scene! John recalls in that chapter Jesus making an outrageous claim: "I am the Bread of Life. He who eats of me shall not hunger. She who drinks of me shall not thirst. And if you eat my very flesh and drink my very blood, you shall have life within you. Forever."

And the crowds who had been gathering and following Jesus, hoping to witness another of his miracles, they hear this and conclude that this itinerant preacher from Galilee has gone stark raving mad! He's simply lost it!

So, as John describes the scene, the crowds ditch Jesus, and soon Jesus is alone, still ranting about the Bread of Life, and suddenly notices that the crowds of people who had been following him had departed. And so Jesus turns to his disciples and asks: "Will you also leave me?"

Peter blurts out: "We would, but where in the heck would we go? Only you have words of Eternal Life!"

I can just hear Maureen blurting out those very same words. She had absolutely no tolerance for any element of religion that did not elevate and lift up the divine in each one of us. And though constantly exasperated with the Catholic Church, it was within the Catholic Church where she always made her home. Like Peter, like it or lump it, the life of the Gospel in the context of the Catholic Church was for Maureen Hallinan, ultimately, the only game in town. So she put up with us, most of the time!

But she did much, much more than that. She embodied the very life of the Eucharist. Whether it was in her life as a religious, or a spouse, or a mother, a friend, a teacher, or a scholar, this restless woman was always feverishly busy finding ways to give her life away. And so, little by little, we witnessed Maureen simply become the Eucharist. (I'm reminded of the grace-filled words of another wonderful friend, Maggie Daley, when she was suffering from a cancer that would claim her life. One day, a family member said to Maggie: "I am so angry that this cancer is taking your life from you!" Maggie responded, "There's nothing that will take my life from me. I'm too busy giving it away.")

And how Maureen gave it away to all of us, all the time. First, with her beloved Chris and Renee, and oh what a thunderous grace when her grandchild, little Thomas, arrived. Maureen just beamed with utter joy in the presence of her children and grandchild. And in their presence, this prodigious scholar and intellect would melt and become childlike herself. Likewise, she gave her life away to her friends, with her gentle teasing, her mischievous surprises, her love of life and of the simplest of pleasures.

So, as we remember and celebrate the life of this remarkably holy woman, we gratefully acknowledge the gift that God has shared with us. Maureen finally possesses the answers she so tirelessly sought. She can now simply rest in the arms of this elusive and mysterious God she pursued and hounded so relentlessly every day of her life.

I can't help but ponder: how is God going to handle having Maureen around? I wish God luck on this one, since God is gonna have a handful! I'll bet God's getting that famous *glare* right now, and that Maureen has already been demanding some explanations!

For our part, the ones left behind for now, though we will miss Maureen terribly, our lives have been changed, and endlessly enriched, by her presence. She has become the Eucharist, and we take comfort in the sure and certain hope that she now forms in an even more intimate way, the Body of the resurrected Christ. Forever!

Rev. Timothy R. Scully, C.S.C.

Acknowledgments

This project came when I was at a low point in my life. I wanted to write a book on spirituality, but I was physically ill and lacked the energy and strength. At the same time, I had the good fortune to work with Ann Berends, and we agreed to do this project together. Ann was filled with joy and talent, generosity and good ideas. This book would not have been written without her daily assistance. So it is with deep gratitude that I acknowledge her here.

Thank you to those who read earlier drafts of this book: John, Tom, and Rita; Christopher and Renee; Tim Scully; Sonia Gernes; and June Primus. Your input was invaluable.

My thanks to members of the Institute for Educational Initiatives and the Alliance for Catholic Education, who were kind to me during this process. Tim Scully was an enthusiastic support from the beginning. Joyce Johnstone came over again and again to see how she could help. Tom Doyle and John Staud attempted to use their profound gardening skills to create a bird sanctuary outside the window of my apartment (a sanctuary that was unceremoniously dismantled by the squirrels).

Mark Berends frequently brought me lunch and the warmth of his company.

My daughter Renee has been my dedicated ally, chauffeur, and escort. Christopher has taken on the logistical challenges of my illness. He, Carrie, and Thomas never fail to cheer me when they walk through the door. I am grateful to my children for their love and their presence. They are the greatest gifts from God to me.

Bibliography

Cross, John of the. *The Living Flame of Love* (Stanza 3: 30). New York, NY: Cosimo, 1912. p. 75

Cross, John of the. *Ascent of Mount Carmel* (Book 2, Chapter 19). Christian Classics Ethereal Library. n.d. Web. 15 Jan. 2014.

Cross, John of the. *A Spiritual Canticle of the Soul* (Book 1.16-17). Christian Classics Ethereal Library,. n.d. Web. 15 Jan. 2014.

Cross, John of the. *The Works of Saint John of the Cross.* Catholic Spiritual Direction, n.d. Letter 20: To a Carmelite Nun. Web. 15 Jan. 2014.

Merton, Thomas. *Conjectures of a Guilty Bystander.* Garden City, NY: Doubleday, 1966. p. 206.

Merton, Thomas. *Thoughts in Solitude.* New York, NY: Farrer, Straus and Cudahay, 1999. p. 33

Merton, Thomas. *Life Free from Care.* n.d. Web. 15 Jan. 2014.

Permissions

References

Griffin, John Howard. *Black Like Me.* Boston: Houghton Mifflin, 1961.

Hazard, David. *You Set My Spirit Free: A 40-Day Journey in the Company of John of the Cross.* Minneapolis, MN: Bethany House. 1994.

Matthew, Iain. *The Impact of God: Soundings from John of the Cross.* London: Hodder and Stoughton. 1995.

Merton, Thomas. *No Man is an Island.* New York, NY: Fall River Press. 2003.